GONE FERAL

ALSO BY NOVELLA CARPENTER

Farm City

The Essential Urban Farmer
with Willow Rosenthal

GONE FERAL

Tracking My Dad Through the Wild

―

NOVELLA CARPENTER

THE PENGUIN PRESS

New York

2014

THE PENGUIN PRESS
Published by the Penguin Group
Penguin Group (USA) LLC
375 Hudson Street
New York, New York 10014

USA · Canada · UK · Ireland · Australia
New Zealand · India · South Africa · China

penguin.com
A Penguin Random House Company

First published by The Penguin Press,
a member of Penguin Group (USA) LLC, 2014

LIBRARY OF CONGRESS CATALOGING-IN-PUBLICATION DATA
Carpenter, Novella, 1972-
Gone feral : tracking my dad through the wild / Novella Carpenter.
p.   cm.
ISBN 978-1-59420-443-2
1. Fathers and daughters—Idaho.   2. Interpersonal relations—Idaho.
3. Missing persons—Idaho.   I. Title.
HQ755.85C3597   2014   2013039981
306.874'2—dc23

Printed in the United States of America
1   3   5   7   9   10   8   6   4   2

DESIGNED BY AMANDA DEWEY

One of the names and identifying characteristics have been changed
to protect the privacy of the individual involved.

For my sister, Riana,
who always seems to know

Contents

PART I

—

MISSING

Dad holding one-year-old baby Novella on the ranch in
Idaho. The funky trailer in the background was
home sweet home, 1973.

One

My dad officially went missing on October 17, 2009.

The morning I found out, I woke up to the hum of traffic from Interstate 980 harmonizing with the nickering of milk goats at my back stairs. I made a cup of Lapsang souchong tea and got ready for a morning of manure shoveling out in my Oakland farm. I threw on my jeans and a stained T-shirt worn the day before and sat down to put on a pair of cowgirl boots that I had bought years ago at a feed store in Texas. The salesgirl promised the boots would give me superior stirrup control. I bought them without mentioning that I was an urban cowgirl, and that the only horse I ever rode was a bicycle. As I pulled on the boots, I noticed my phone on the kitchen table, blinking with a message.

"Hi, Novella, this is your mom, and you're probably on your way someplace," she started, cautious. Her voice sounded flittery and nervous, not her usual upbeat tone. Listening, I could just see her, sitting in her favorite old leather chair, a

Guatemalan pillow propped behind her back, her long blond-gray hair pulled back in a side ponytail—a holdover from her hippie days.

"But I just—Barb just called me." Barb, one of my mom's friends from back in her Idaho homesteading years. "She said there was an article in the Orofino paper saying . . . ah . . . local man reported missing and"—there was a dramatic pause—"it's your dad."

My heart shrank as she went on. "It's very peculiar, it said he was last seen on the seventeenth. Give me a call or e-mail. Weird, huh? OK, talk to you later."

It was October 23. He had been missing for six days. I punched in my mom's phone number. It rang once. Twice. Three times. Four. She has multiple sclerosis and walks with a cane, so it takes her awhile to get to the phone.

"Hello?" she answered finally.

"Hi, Mom, it's Novella," I said. "Dad's missing?"

Her voice deepened conspiratorially. "So you haven't heard from him?"

"No," I answered. I felt sick.

"Well, Barb said she saw it in the paper," she repeated.

"Maybe he went to France?" I ventured, remembering that Dad had recently sent my sister, Riana, who lives outside of Narbonne, a cryptic e-mail about a "farewell" trip to France. Suddenly the word *farewell* seemed kind of ominous.

"Well, he is getting older," my mother started. An image came to me: The verdant woods of Idaho, a chilly morning with mist creeping through a dense thicket of trees. A lonely truck on the side of a gray-rock road. My dad, wearing cowboys boots and a pair of worn Levi's, collapsed on the forest floor. Chainsaw in one hand, his eyes staring up into the sky, vacant.

A thought flitted by: *outliving Dad might be a bit of a triumph for Mom.*

They met in 1969. After some adventures in Europe, they bought a 180-acre ranch in Idaho. Raise their own food, make babies, and live the good life—that was their hope. But by 1976, only a few years in, the marriage was over, a shit storm of shattered ideals.

"We're all getting older," I snapped, suddenly annoyed. "He's in better shape than me!" Unlike my mom, who moved to town and got a real job as a schoolteacher, my dad retreated farther into the woods. As far as I knew, he was still making a living off the land like some kind of mountain man. The last time I had seen him, more than three years ago, he had been hale and hearty as a wood sprite.

"OK, OK," she said, sensing my panic. Mom said goodbye and promised to call if she heard anything. I fetched my tea and leaned against the kitchen counter and took a swig. Then I clomped into the living room. One wall was lined with a sagging shelf of vinyl records, the mantle above our defunct fireplace was cluttered with a pair of deer horns, a hummingbird nest, and an old, metal milk-ration ladle from World War II–era France. I fished out my laptop, buried under some newspapers and books, and looked up "Orofino newspaper."

Orofino is a sleepy little town in the panhandle of Idaho. My birthplace. Only a few thousand people live there—I didn't know Orofino even had a newspaper. But there it was: the *Clearwater Tribune*, named after the Clearwater River that runs by the funky little burg. Sandwiched between notices about flu season and an announcement for the Orofino Community choir practice was the news report about my missing dad.

Missing man not seen since Oct. 17

George E. Carpenter, age 73, has not been seen since Saturday morning, Oct. 17. George is known to cut firewood in the area north of Rudo Road. George drives a 1996 Ford F-150 pickup with license plate 6C 17470. He is 5'10" tall, weighs 175 pounds, and has gray hair and brown eyes. If anyone has seen him or has knowledge of his whereabouts, please contact the Clearwater County Sheriff's Office at (208) 476-4521.

Dad was seventy-three years old. I didn't want to think about it any more than I wanted to recognize that I was now thirty-six, the same age as my dad when he first held me as a newborn on a snowy December night in Idaho. Thirty-six, an age when you start catching glimpses of mortality: gray hairs and crow's feet; worries about ailing, aged parents.

Rudo Road—I had no idea where that was. The only road in Orofino that I knew by name was the Gilbert Grade, where my parents' ranch had been. They divorced when I was four, and Dad mostly disappeared from my life. The *Clearwater Tribune*'s headline—MISSING MAN—simply made it official. To be missing, lost, out of sight: that was my dad's natural state.

I had always accepted, or at least didn't dwell on, his absence, but now that he had disappeared in such a dramatic, tangible way, I felt compelled to find him. I called the Clearwater County Sheriff's office. Before long, I was talking to a police officer who sounded young enough to be in high school.

"I'm George Carpenter's daughter," I said into the phone. "I heard he's missing."

"Yes," the officer said, immediately getting down to business. "He usually plays pool with friends in the morning, and he hasn't showed up in a few days."

Pool in the morning? Only in Idaho. "Did you find his truck?" I knew that he often drove to Arizona for the winter, to a small western town called Wickenburg, where he waited out the harsh Orofino winter. My mom thought this migration pattern was ironic: "Your dad used to say, 'mountain man's always planning for the winter,'" she would scoff. "Now he's a snowbird!"

If the police had found his truck, he surely must be dead. I clenched my stomach while I waited for her response.

"No," she said, and I felt a wave of relief. She continued, "But a neighbor called to say he saw George's guitar inside his cabin and the door was wide open." My heart plunged. He wouldn't leave his guitar, which he had built with his own hands out of Idaho rosewood. The open door seemed sinister. Maybe, I thought, he had been diagnosed with some terminal illness? If so, would he end it with a shotgun, just like his hero, Hemingway?

The cop cleared her throat. "We're on a manhunt for him now."

"I should say that—ah—we're kind of estranged," I confessed, then picked up a broom and started sweeping the kitchen. "We don't really talk."

"How do you usually communicate?" she asked.

"E-mail," I said, my voice catching at our pathetic form of communication.

"I have his phone number," she said.

"Can I get it?" I asked, astonished that he had a phone. I didn't think he even had electricity.

"Let me make sure—I don't want to give it out if it's unlisted." She paused for a minute and I heard some shuffling and clicking. Then she was back and said, "OK, it's listed." I put my broom down and picked up a pen. She gave me the number, which I wrote on the back of my hand, suddenly self-conscious that I didn't have my own father's phone number.

"Let us know if you hear from him," she said. "He's not in trouble, but we need to find him. We've already spent a hundred man hours looking."

I hung up the phone and took a deep breath.

I dialed the phone number written on the back of my hand. I'd never been to my dad's house, but I imagined a rustic cabin a la Walden, hand-built and simple, tucked under a grove of evergreens. The little chimney wasn't puffing out smoke, though, the river rock fireplace must have been empty and cold. The telephone, which surely must be a rotary was dead too; a computerized woman's voice came on, saying, "We're sorry, but this number has been disconnected. We're sorry, but this number has been disconnected."

Later that evening, I found myself scanning the bookshelves, trying to find a book Dad sent me long ago, when my cell phone rang. It was my sister, Riana, calling from France, where it was very early in the morning. Mom had alerted her about Dad.

"I just got off the phone with the Orofino Sheriff's office," Riana said. She was almost breathless. She's blond, willow thin, and tall. We have the same jutting chin and large, owl-like eyes. We are sometimes mistaken for twins, but unlike me with my crooked teeth and big honker nose, Riana has straight teeth and a pert, freckled nose.

"Did you talk to that young girl officer?" I asked.

"Yeah." This continuity made me feel calm. The girl cop

is there, all day long, working on the case, following leads, goddammit.

We were both quiet for a minute. My sister is two years older than me, so she remembers more about Dad. She has also claimed to be clairvoyant. I waited for her analysis, holding my breath.

"My feeling is he's in Arizona," she said after a long pause.

I let out my breath, nodded. "Yeah."

"But why would he leave his guitar?" I asked her. He was a devoted classical guitar player. His postcards always mentioned that he was collecting guitar wood to build instruments. If he was driving to Arizona, why not take the guitar with him?

"Maybe he *is* coming to France!?" she shouted.

Riana, her French husband, Benji, and their daughter, Amaya, live in an ancient stone farmhouse in the southwest of France. Like me, my sister grows vegetables, keeps chickens and goats. Dad had been promising to visit her, but so far he hadn't arrived. The idea of our hermit dad taking a fourteen-hour airplane ride to France seemed unlikely, yet my sister and I were ready to believe that he could be on his way to her house right now. Perhaps, I thought, he had found a slow boat to France and would be hiking into my sister's tiny village, Jean Valjean style. Hope, in the case of our father, springs eternal—despite all evidence to the contrary.

"Could be," I said. "But does he even have enough money to get out of Idaho?"

"So true," she said. He was always broke.

"I'm glad I at least got to see him," Riana said. Last year, Riana and Benji had flown to Idaho to see Dad, and introduce him to Amaya, his granddaughter, who was one and a half years old back then.

The trip had been a bit of a disaster. Dad picked them up at the airport in Lewiston, then spent an hour driving around before dropping them off at a hotel in Orofino. The next day he was so dodgy he didn't want to go to his house. Instead he took them out for hamburgers, then deposited them back at the hotel. Stunned, but trying to make the best of it, Riana and Benji entertained Amaya by wading in the Clearwater River. Riana picked through the rocks along the shore, hoping to find some arrowheads left by the local Indian tribe, the Nez Percé. They left for Montana the next day.

"At least Amaya got to meet her grandpa," I said glumly.

My sister and I promised to call each other the moment we heard anything, and we hung up.

From the backyard, I heard the goats snort, followed by the sound of my boyfriend, Bill, riding his bike into the backyard, home after a day's work at the garage. I went outside and peered over the railing. Our backyard is a bit of old Appalachia in Oakland. There's a rickety goat shed, a wobbly clothesline, an outhouse constructed out of old signboards, and a falling-down flight of stairs that leads up to our apartment. I could see Bill locking his bike to a half-rotted fence post, our goats nibbling on the back of his T-shirt.

"Billy!" I yelled. He smiled up at me and started walking slowly up the back stairs. His thick dark hair stood on end; his face was covered with engine oil. He wore a thrashed pair of Carhartt work pants, and his black T-shirt was shredded so that you could see bits of his hairy belly peeking out. We've been together eleven years, since 1998, when we met in an elevator in Seattle. He has soulful brown-gold eyes and long eyelashes that he hides behind big glasses. He walks with a limp, and has chronic back pain from wrestling cars all day.

"My dad's missing," I said when he reached me.

"Shit," he muttered, his voice tattered and grumbly from years of chain smoking. He gave me a hug and sniffed my hair. He smelled like brake cleaner and sweat from his bike ride. The goats followed him upstairs and milled between our legs on the back porch.

"They're having a manhunt for him," I reported. I wondered exactly what a manhunt in Orofino looked like. Did they have four-by-four vehicles going off-road, tracking him like a wild animal? Or was it more like driving around, chewing tobacco and shooting the shit? The police officer said one hundred man hours, but did that include stops for coffee and donuts?

We went inside to cook supper and brainstorm about what could have happened. Bill had a special fondness for my dad. He first met him in Arizona, at a fleabag apartment where my dad had holed up for the winter. Over the years, Bill has seen him again a few other times, during sporadic father-daughter visits. To Bill, my dad's off-the-grid lifestyle felt fresh and unpredictable.

Bill's hunch about the whereabouts of my dad: truck problems. I told him that the newspaper said Dad drove a 1996 Ford truck. "His truck is old, so . . ." Bill began. "Or he's probably stuck in a ditch somewhere." He shambled off to take a hot bath and read before bed. Car trouble, not dead in the woods. It was a reassuring thought.

After supper I went back into our guestroom and found the book I had been looking for. It was crammed in a corner of the shelf, between *Breaking Out of Beginner's Spanish* and a *Chilton's* guide: *Pan*, by Knut Hamsun. I pulled it off the shelf. The cover featured a red-horned goat-man. My dad sent it to me years earlier, in 1991, during my first quarter at the University of Washington in Seattle. Back then I felt like I had finally escaped, had gotten away from the logging town where I grew up. I was eighteen and had discovered something called art-house movies, and, like everyone else in town, was excited about a local band called Nirvana. In the dorm mail room I opened up the package from my dad with trepidation. Before leaving for college, I had sent Dad a bitchy letter, upbraiding him for various things, but mostly for not helping me pay for tuition. In reaction, Dad—or Pops or Papa, as he liked to call himself—had sent me this item. Tucked inside the worn and reused packaging was the novel *Pan*. A note scribbled on the back of an envelope said, "This book sums up my philosophy of life!" I felt relieved there was no bitchy counter-letter, but annoyed there was no money in the envelope either. When I took the time to read *Pan*—a book about a hermit hunter who lives in a remote cabin—I just couldn't, or didn't want to, relate.

Years later, after I had become an idealistic environmentalist, toting a metal coffee mug at all times, living in big group houses, and not shaving my legs (somehow, I thought, this behavior might help old-growth forests and save the northern spotted owl), I devoured *Pan*. Hamsun had captured the beauty of nature, and of man's struggle to keep wilderness alive, even as society encroached. I didn't want to live in the woods, but I was proud that my dad had made that choice. I've moved many times over the years, deserting most of my possessions, save for my journals and a handful of precious books, *Pan* being key among them.

The night I found out Dad had gone missing, I read *Pan* for the first time in years. I stopped every so often to check my e-mail, knowing that nothing would come from Dad unless he had somehow stumbled across a twenty-four-hour library with Internet access. *Pan* tells the story of a woodsman hunter named Lieutenant Glahn. Glahn is more wild animal than man. He shoots birds for a living, wears simple leather clothes, and is socially awkward and unpredictable.

"I did not go hunting just to be able to shoot things but to enable me to live in the forest," Glahn narrates. "It suited me there; I lay on the ground for my meals and did not have to sit bolt upright on a chair. . . . In the forest I did as I liked." I couldn't help but notice how much Glahn resembled my dad—or at least what I thought my dad was like. He lived in the forest, solitary, doing what he wanted. Around three in the morning, as I turned the last pages, I suddenly remembered how the book ends: Glahn dead, shot, in the woods.

The next morning I called my goat up for morning milking. As I leaned into her warm flanks, drawing out the milk, I wondered if I would be going to Idaho to clean out my dead dad's cabin. Would that be my chance to finally stitch together who he was—and what he had been doing—for all these missing years? The thought chilled me.

I poured the goat milk through a filter and stashed the jars in the fridge. Then I checked my e-mail. A message had come:

> hi sweets, all well on the western front, i'm here in
> wickenburg, az; thanks for your concern . . . guitar #10—
> the benji–ri—is getting my love daily—sorry to have caused
> any upset; reading hemingway my dream visitor
>> love you always,
>> papa

Papa. That old goat!

I forwarded his e-mail to my sister and Mom. Of course he was OK. He always bragged that he had nine lives, just like a cat.

Gnawing in the back of my brain, though, was a little rodent of doubt. He has been missing most of my life, and now he was getting older. Though he had emerged unscathed, what about the next time? What happened when he ran out of lives?

Dad on the Clearwater River, where my parents camped,
just before buying the 180-acre ranch in Orofino, 1971.

Two

Bill was asleep when I went into our bedroom to tell him the good news that my dad had resurfaced in Wickenburg, probably shacked up at the Purple Hills Apartments again. Our room was dark, womb-like. I had painted it midnight blue when we first moved in, back in 2003. We had left Seattle that year, fleeing the rain and looking for jobs. We picked Oakland because we liked its wild west vibe, and settled in a scruffy neighborhood the locals called Ghost Town.

A plain mattress lay on the floor. On the milk crate that serves as our night table, an apple core and several Q-tips lay fanned out.

"Monk," I whispered. *Monkey*, or *monk*, I'm embarrassed to admit, is our nickname for each other. Monkey number 1 and 2. That and *dog*. I yanked on the comforter Bill had cocooned himself in.

"Time is it?" he mumbled. His breath smelled like dead flowers.

"Ten," I said. Practically dawn for Bill—he loves to sleep in and stay up late at night. He peered out from under the covers. His hair was crumpled on one side and stood on end on the other, Medusa-like.

"Dad's OK," I said. "In Arizona."

"That's nice," he muttered.

I gave Bill a kiss and left him to sleep a few hours longer. I bundled up in a garish floral scarf and a fake-fur hat. Tucking a pair of Felco pruners in my back pocket, I swung my leg across an old blue mountain bike and rode north. It had rained the day before, so it was a perfect time to go on a collecting mission to find branches to feed the goats. The wind was cold and bracing. As I rode, I felt a vague sense of unease.

I should have been happy. Bill loved me. We had lots of friends. My family was fine, even Dad. Our farm was thriving. Just a few weeks before Dad had gone missing, Bill and I had begun trying to get pregnant, and now I was a few days late. I might be pregnant.

A fine mist in the air speckled my glasses. I dodged Oakland's broken glass and potholes until I rode into Berkeley, turning down a street lined with liquidambar trees. The chill of October had turned the leaves of the trees a deep red. I pulled my bike over to a tree with a broken branch, grabbed the end of it, and yanked it down. I cut up the limb into smaller branches and secured them to my bike basket with a bit of baling twine, and rode home, the leaves rustling. At my house I parked my bike and called to my caprine family.

The herd (Nigerian Dwarf goats, a mini-breed ideal for backyard farms) clattered down the stairs. I threw the branches into a manger I had made by lashing together a pair of metal window bars that had once been installed inside our apartment to protect against burglars. Having bars both outside and *inside* seemed extreme, even in our somewhat sketchy neighborhood.

While the goats ate, I sat on the stairs. I breathed in the mild scent of wet wood chips, the light low and gray. A golden kid with blue eyes that I had named Milky Way leaped into my lap and curled down for a nap. I sniffed her head, which smelled like chèvre. I pulled the goatling in close, toward my stomach, which felt twitchy and weird. I hadn't told Mom about my new breeding plan. I definitely hadn't told Dad. Would he even care? I wasn't sure, but I knew that before I tried to start a family of my own, I needed to try to make things right with Dad.

The last time I had seen him was in Idaho, in 2006. I had taken a summer-long newspaper reporting gig in the Gem State. I was thirty-two; Bill and I had been living in Oakland for a few years by then. Somehow I had gotten into graduate school at UC Berkeley. I was studying journalism, but was still trying to figure out what to do with my life.

I chose the internship in Idaho because of Dad. He lived only a few hours from where I would be stationed at the *Post Register* in Idaho Falls. I hadn't seen him since 2001, when we had one of our usual brief and unsatisfying one-hour-long reunions, which usually involved an awkward lunch, followed by hugs and empty I-Love-Yous. By coming to Idaho, I was hoping to draw him out for some substantial contact. If I appeared on his turf, I figured he wouldn't be able to resist seeing me.

With that idea, I packed a few things into our rusty 1976 Mercedes Benz and headed north. It was June. Bill stayed behind in Oakland to take care of our apartment and the farm

we had built together. On the farmlette, in addition to vegetables and fruit trees, we raised egg-laying chickens, honey-
bees, turkeys, ducks, rabbits, and even pigs once, though that
nearly killed us. As I drove away from our little urban farm,
the Bay Area fell away to the hot Sacramento Delta, then into
the verdant Willamette Valley. I followed the Columbia River
because the car couldn't make it over any major mountain
passes.

Driving my beater car into Idaho had been like a homecom-
ing. I still thought of it as my home state even though I hadn't
lived there in decades. I cruised past wild forests that seemed
to go on forever, then stopped in a funky roadside diner for eggs
and coffee. Back on the road, a man wearing goggles and a
leather flight cap passed by me in a convertible he had obviously
built himself out of scrap parts, with custom mufflers and Idaho
plates. Funky, wild, hacked—this is Idaho.

Idaho Falls, the town I was assigned, didn't quite have the
scruffy feel of where I was raised, up in northern Idaho. Idaho
Falls had lots of American flags waving from porches of well-
kept homes. A river ran through the village, making a lazy
progression to the falls where an enormous Mormon Temple
sprouted up, looking like a wedding cake decoration. Exploring the tidy little town, I walked by a bar that harbored the
old Idaho spirit that I had remembered—next to the neon
Budweiser sign in the window, a handwritten note had been
posted: *If you have been 86'ed here, you are still 86'ed.*

Not far from the bar, I found a cheap apartment. It had
orange shag carpet and a Murphy bed. I unpacked my suit-
case, found a coffee shop, and settled in. I sent word to Dad
that I was in state and waited for a response. Like anyone
working for a podunk newspaper in the middle of Idaho, I

read Norman Maclean's *A River Runs Through It*, and heavily romanticized my new job—and fly-fishing.

I covered the police beat and spent most of my days trolling the cop shop for stories. I listened to the police radio night and day like my hero, crime reporter Edna Buchanan. I was hoping for a juicy story. Sometimes there were: a nurse caught selling oxytocin, a man accused of attempted strangulation. But most days were slow, and I found myself covering events like the hot-air balloon festival or the Fourth of July parade. As the summer progressed, I was accepted into the newsroom as a decent reporter. Not a peep from Dad, though.

One day my editor, a lanky guy named Dean, gathered me and a few other reporters into his car and took us out to a farmer's field. He opened up the hatchback of his Subaru and yanked off a camo blanket to display a gleaming arsenal of guns. Shotguns and old-timey revolvers, Glocks and rifles. Dean thought I should know about firearms if I was going to cover crime. He jogged into the hills with paper targets shaped like men and set them up at different distances. I clamped on some ear protection and began blowing away the paper targets. It was really fun. I had used firearms before—my dad had showed me how to use a shotgun when I was so young the kickback of the rifle sent me onto my ass. Later, in rural Washington State, I had attended a middle school that had target practice as an elective. Still, I had never fired a 9 millimeter before, and I couldn't believe how much power one small weapon could contain. The editor's wife came along for shooting practice and told me women have better aim than men. She once shot and field dressed an elk by herself, lugged the meat to her truck, and a few weeks later gave birth to their third child.

As I stood there, heart pounding from the raw power of the gleaming Glock, I thought about my friend who had gotten an internship at the *New York Times*. He was probably seated in a conference room with a view of the Manhattan skyline, surrounded by seasoned *Times* reporters. My friend was making connections, reporting on real crime, setting up his future career. Meanwhile, here I was in a field in Idaho, blowing away targets, waiting to hear from my estranged dad.

He didn't show, and it turned out to be a lonely summer. It felt like I was marooned in Idaho Falls. I missed Billy, and cried when one night his voice cracked on the phone when he said "I love you too." I also, idiotically, missed my rice cooker.

I decided that if I wasn't going to see my dad, I could at least get close to him by proxy: by going camping and enjoying the outdoors. When I was just a kid he used to point out edible wild plants to me and my sister. One time, when Riana was five and I was three, Dad showed us a flush of morel mushrooms erupting under a grove of wild apple trees on the ranch where we grew up. They were wrinkled, penis-like, and smelled like meaty forest.

When I was much older he gave me a copy Euell Gibbons's *Stalking the Wild Asparagus*. First published in 1962, the book had become a cult classic for the back-to-nature crowd of my parents' generation. When he gave me the book he told me that he and Mom had used it as a guide to prepare wild food on their ranch. They made flour out of cattails that grew in the duck pond, and steeped a tea of pine boughs to keep warm in the winter.

Remembering these stories, I had thrown *Stalking* in the trunk of my car and took it with me to Idaho Falls. There, after work most nights, I followed the book's directions to forage things like crab apples and wild mustard greens. I hunted young milkweed pods in an abandoned field. I steamed them with butter, and they tasted better than any domesticated vegetable I had ever eaten.

Dad gave me *Stalking the Wild Asparagus* with one caveat, though. Euell had eventually become a spokesman for a breakfast cereal company. "Goddamn Grape Nuts," Dad moaned. A warning to never sell out.

On one of my few weekends off from the *Post Register*, I embarked on my first solo backpacking trip. Even though I consider myself an environmentalist, I always thought the best way to save the wild was to leave it alone. I packed a gallon of water, some sardines, and a loaf of rye bread, and tried to channel my father by hiking ten miles up a mountain. Dad, I imagined, would have easily hiked up the steep trail, and probably would have trapped a small mammal to spit roast on an open fire.

I, on the other hand, became immediately breathless and sweaty once I started hiking. Halfway up the trail, I was completely spent and couldn't make it to the campsite. Instead, I slept under a ponderosa pine. Gazing up at the cloudy night sky, I felt peaceful, proud of myself even, but also so lonely. In the middle of the night a storm rolled in, so I built a little shelter out of branches to block the rain.

The next morning I woke up with a sticky resin glommed to the side of my face and pieces of bark snagged in my hair. My entire body ached. The hike down was thrillingly beautiful, though: the blue lupine flowers were pebbled with moisture, and Queen Anne's lace majestically rose up along the trail, sending out a carroty, bitter smell. It was August, and the beauty all around me did lift my heart. As I hiked, I sang songs to myself to stave off the loneliness and the terrible feeling of the summer being over and sensing it was a time for change, but not knowing what the hell I was doing with my life.

I returned to my Idaho Falls apartment and my job. Then, finally, I got an e-mail from Dad. He wrote that he was coming and would be there the next day. And he was bringing his fly-fishing gear.

"Novella, you have a visitor," Peggy, the front desk lady, called to tell me over the phone, though the office was small enough that I could hear her without amplification. I was working on an important story about the city's new dog-poop ordinance.

I came out from my cubicle and there he was. He was lean and wore a dirty beige cowboy hat, a worn pair of Levi's, and a Pendleton wool shirt I had sent him for Christmas ten years before.

"Hey, sweets!" he yelled. He gave me a hug and a kiss. He had an elfin expression on his face, brown eyes shining, pointy chin pointing. He looked fit as a fiddle.

"This is quite a place," he said, surveying my ratty office. "This is big time! I'll be damned." I guessed that he hadn't been to many offices before. I wasn't sure what he was impressed by—the flimsy press board desks? The ancient computers? He let out a hoot and gave me another hug.

That night we went to Fred Meyer and bought fishing licenses, then split the prime rib special meal at a restaurant called Fish and Steak. I told him about my summer, what I liked about Idaho, how the farm in Oakland was progressing. I felt a little uneasy being with him. I hadn't seen him in five years, since the quick, hour-long visit when I was living in Seattle and he had come to town for some reason. I was glad we had an activity—fly-fishing—to focus on.

Though I had a perfectly good couch, when we got back to my apartment that night he settled into my closet to sleep. There he made a nest of couch pillows and a sleeping bag. In the middle of the night, I woke up to the sound of some rustling: it was Dad getting up to go to the bathroom. I heard him quietly muttering, "Jesus, Jesus," as he peed. The next morning, when I woke up, his sleeping bag was still in the closet, but he was nowhere to be found.

"Dad?" I called and looked in the kitchen. Nobody in there. I prepared myself for the inevitable—he had left, it had been too intense seeing me, and, as usual, he'd bailed.

Then I heard it: music, slightly muffled. I looked out the window of my apartment, through the vibrant green leaves of the plane trees. I saw Dad sitting in the passenger seat of his dingy blue Geo Metro. The door was ajar. One cowboy-boot-clad foot rested on the curb. He was playing his guitar.

Seeing him there made me think, suddenly, of my first memory of him. I must have been about three. I woke up next to my sister in the low bed we shared upstairs in the half-finished, wholly unpermitted house my parents had been building for years on their ranch in Idaho. An enormous half-circle window of the sort that was popular in certain hippie circles in the 1970s let in the dawn light. I reached for my copy of Dr. Seuss's *The Foot Book*. Someone had left the book in the root cellar one winter, and the pages were spotted with mold. I couldn't read yet, but I had memorized it, and was starting to see a pattern with the words. "Wet foot/Dry foot," I said to myself.

My young ears heard a chair scrape across the tile floor. Dad coughed once, and then a deep bass of a guitar chord resonated through the half-empty house. The music was haunting and slow. Dad stopped playing and did some tun-

ing, then resumed. I crept out of my bed onto the rough ply-
wood floor, and peered through a jagged cut-out in the
drywall that was one day going to be a heater vent. Down in
the living room, Dad was seated in a beam of sunlight. He
was perched near the picture windows filled with the scrubby
golden hills of northern Idaho. He was cradling his guitar in
his arms. A cup of coffee sat beside his foot, a curl of smoke
rising from it. His eyes closed as he started playing Bach's
"Jesu, Joy of Man's Desiring." I went back to my bed to read
but I heard him occasionally stop to replay notes, back up, and
start over again. Then the guitar stopped, the front door
opened and closed, and he was gone, out to work in the woods
cruising timber.

So many years had passed—could it really be over thirty?—
and there I was, standing in my Idaho Falls apartment, my
toes in the orange shag carpet, listening to him again. I un-
wound the stove-top espresso maker, packed it with coffee,
and turned on the flame. When it was ready, I brought some
coffee down to the car.

"My studio," he said as I handed him the mug, and
grinned. After breakfast, we headed out to the river.

It wasn't a good year for fishing. The drought had dried
up all but the biggest rivers, but we wanted to try anyway, and
the outdoors reporter at the newspaper told us of a spot.

"You get a reel and I'll get a pole," Dad sang on the way to
the river, "and we'll head on down to the fishing hole . . ." He
was like a little bird, chirping and whistling, not talking about
anything important, just being.

The spot was called Ririe. There was an impressive stand
of cottonwood trees along the river that cast a refreshing

shade. The river was wide but shallow, rippling across flat river rocks. I was no fly-fishing expert, but it looked pretty perfect to me. We parked in a gravel parking lot and carried our gear down a steep path to the river. It was hot, and grasshoppers dodged our feet. A slow canal ran along the path. There was another fisherman there, throwing his line in, when we arrived. Dad barely looked at him and started setting up nearby.

"This'll be tender as an old maid's first kiss," he said, choosing a fly from his tackle box, then tying it to the end of the line. He is a master of the colorful metaphor. A few of his best sayings: It was raining like a cow pissing on a flat rock, or It's as cold as an Eskimo fart.

The fly in his hand was a commercial fly called a Rooster Tail. I was a little disappointed that he didn't tie his own like Paul in *A River Runs Through It*. He showed me how to attach the fly to the line, and the hidden hook that would get lodged in the trout's mouth. I didn't know about fishing etiquette, so I wasn't sure we should be so close to another fisherman, but my dad seemed unfazed and showed me how to cast. The rod had a cork handle.

"It's not your wrist," he instructed. "You use your whole arm, so it's an extension." He cast to show me. The line swirled in the air, once, twice, and then softly landed, like a real insect might, in the middle of the shallow river. He started reeling in, pulling gently so the fly danced across the top of the water. I liked the motion of fly-fishing, and the idea that we were trying to fool a fish. Dad was wearing a white sweater and a baseball cap; he looked nothing like the man next to us, with his official-seeming fly-fishing khakis and multi-pocketed vest.

We were fishing for trout—rainbows, cutthroat, or browns.

Dad showed me how to cast a few times, whistling and casting, then pulling the line in slowly. He watched the current of the river and aimed for the quiet spots. He was relaxed and spry, utterly in his element. The uneasy feeling I had from the night before disappeared. The man next to us stopped fishing and watched Dad. His athletic casting was a thing of beauty. My heart swelled with pride—he was like Paul in *A River Runs Through It*!

We had only one pole, so after half an hour of instruction, I had my chance to cast. He had made it look easy—but my first cast sent the line into the reeds along the river. Startled, I pulled too hard, and the line snapped. The fly was lost. I felt horrible.

"It's OK, babes," he said when he saw my stricken expression. Looking for a better spot, we picked our way to the edge of the canal. He tied on another fly. He pointed out ripples on the surface of the water and I cast. And cast again. And cast again. I was getting the hang of it but I sensed Dad was bored with my amateur attempts. So I handed him the rod, sat on the grass, and admired Dad in his element.

The day had gotten hot, so he had taken off his sweater and stood there in a gray T-shirt. He didn't have a belly like most older men: His stomach was flat, his arms were tanned, and when he pulled the fishing rod back, his biceps bulged. He was wearing Levi's, and like mine they sagged in the butt. Apparently having no ass is hereditary. His dark eyes were narrowed in concentration, scanning the water for the perfect spot. Every once in a while he would stroke his nose, which had flaring, Napoleonic nostrils. He paced along the river bank with the bandy stance of a cowboy, making cast after cast.

Dad told me that he had learned to fish in Hillsboro, Oregon, when he was a young boy. When he was three years old, his father, Fred, had packed the family station wagon, drove south, and never came back. Word came that Fred had started a new family in California. Then, a few months later, he died in a fiery car accident. Dad's mom, my grandmother Jeanne, never quite recovered. She tried to get work as a realtor, but mostly took up drinking and smoking. She foisted her sons—Dad and his older brother—onto her dad, a man everyone called Big George.

Big George was a drinker himself, and a stern taskmaster. He made the boys sleep on stiff cots to build character. It was a kindly neighbor who took my dad and his older brother, Fred Jr., under his wing and showed them how to fish. Seeking escape from their strict grandpa and the ache of their absent parents, the boys would spend whole weekends in the forest near their house exploring, building forts, and pulling crawdads and fish out of a stream that ran through the woods. Years later, Dad's brother went to work for NASA, but died of a heart attack when he was only forty. Dad blamed it on stress, on the rat race.

I watched Dad fish for an hour. His every action had a boyish air, a spryness. It was like I had watched him transform from a craggy mountain hermit into a young man. He didn't catch a trout that day at Ririe but we were happy to have been out in the water, and had built up an appetite.

That night we made dinner at my apartment. We practiced speaking Spanish, which I was learning from a local kid in town. After dinner, I persuaded Dad to play some guitar into my digital recorder. "For Riana, for the new baby," I explained. My sister was pregnant back then with Amaya, due in February.

He went down to his car and fished out his guitar, then

carefully set up a chair in the middle of the room while I fiddled with the digital recorder. I hadn't used it very many times, so I was worried it wouldn't record. He began without warning. It was Bach's "Jesu, Joy of Man's Desiring," the piece I had remembered him practicing when I was a kid. While he played, I noticed his hands were gnarled from his hard life and age, but the music sounded hauntingly beautiful. I kept checking the red light of the recorder, to make sure it was working—that it was capturing the sounds of my past, of my missing father. I recorded a little over three minutes of him playing. I felt triumphant, as if I had bottled a ghost.

He left the next day, leaving me his fishing rod and line, a couple Rooster Tails, and fifty bucks. We had spent almost forty-eight hours together, the biggest chunk of time since I was a little girl. As he drove away, pangs of loneliness welled up in my stomach. Abandoned again.

I had used the rod only one other time. On my last weekend in Idaho Falls I had gone back, alone, to Ririe, where Dad and I had gone fishing. I waded into the cool, shallow water and got a few hard nibbles that were electrifying. That night, I camped out by myself on the rocks high above Ririe. I could see the town's lights twinkling far away. I felt proud of my Idaho summer. I had gone foraging, camping, and tried fly-fishing. I promised myself I would start going on regular fishing trips, that I would finally catch a trout. And I would keep in touch with Dad, build on what we had experienced together. But when I returned to Oakland, back to Bill, back to our farm, I threw the rod in the back room. Eventually, it got covered with garden stuff—floating row cover and old burlap bags—until I could only see the tip of the pole. That brief connection I had with Dad shriveled up and settled into a forgotten corner of my life too.

Now he had reappeared, and it felt like a reminder, a tap on the shoulder. In times past, I probably would have shrugged my shoulders about Dad's close call and his dwindling number of second chances. But this time felt different.

I knew that our chance to have a relationship where he was a caregiver, a nurturer, was long gone. I wondered if there was still an opportunity for something. Maybe friendship. I didn't want to wait until it was too late to reach out to him again. It was time to reckon with the past. Especially now that I was thinking of having a child of my own.

I walked upstairs, sat down at my computer, and crafted an e-mail to my dad, knowing that it might be our last chance.

This whole missing person thing made me realize how much I would regret it if we don't have some meaningful time together. I would love to stay with you and learn some mountain man skills, or just go fly-fishing. I love you dad and love your spirit, I know it flows in me.

Mom holding Novella; Dad with Riana. Bernard,
the steer and chickens in the background, 1974.
Dad calls this era the Good Years.

Three

Mom never responded to the e-mail I forwarded from Dad. Whether she was relieved or disappointed that Dad had turned up alive after the missing person scare, she never told me. My parents had a complicated relationship that ended with outright hostility.

Of course it didn't start like that.

My parents met in Mexico in the spring of 1969, in the gorgeous town of San Miguel de Allende. Dad had hitch-hiked there in search of a guitar maestro, bringing with him only a small leather backpack and his guitar. He set up in a little room in the Quinto Loreto, a cheap crash pad that offered three meals a day and had a tree-lined courtyard where he could play guitar.

After high school, itching to leave Oregon—and his bossy grandfather, who wanted him to work at the family grocery store—my dad joined the army. When he finished his service in 1959 he went to France to learn how to speak French. He was a hungry, disciplined student with an interest in philosophy, especially Sartre. After France, in 1961, he moved to Oakland and enrolled at UC Berkeley. Between classes, he hiked into the Berkeley hills and read books about Native American life. He had a girlfriend who had a guitar hanging on the wall of her living room. One night, he took it down, strummed it—and became enchanted. There was a group of classical and Spanish guitar players in Berkeley at the time, and he gravitated toward them. He learned to play with a devotion that my mom would later call obsessive. Like any good philosophy major, he dropped out of college. He ended up in Central Oregon where he learned how to log and hunt, periodically taking trips like the one to San Miguel de Allende where he met my mom.

Mom graduated from Cal in 1965 with a degree in political science. She had grown up in southern California, in the conservative, wealthy beach town of Corona del Mar. Upon hitting Berkeley, her insular world cracked open. Her professors were activists and were outspoken about the Free Speech Movement on campus. It was a heady time: She went to Vietnam War protests and talked late into the night about the politics of power with her friends. After graduating she stuck around Berkeley to work and continue her political activism. She also traveled: going to Europe, then hitchhiking solo through North Africa. By 1968, after three years of hippie agitating and wanderlust, Mom's spirits were low. Her heroes, Bobby Kennedy and Martin Luther King Jr., were both killed that year. The whole scene was being co-opted too, with tour buses driving through San Francisco's Haight district so tourists could get a look at a real, live hippie. Junkies and freeloaders had shown up, looking for a little bit of free love without the good vibes. So in early 1969, when Mom's friend Dixie invited her to drive to Mexico, Mom didn't hesitate. She jumped into Dixie's VW and they headed south.

Dixie and Mom spent a few weeks driving down the coast before heading inland to the hippie oasis of San Miguel de Allende. Mom fell in love with the colonial town, with its cobblestone streets and bougainvillea growing everywhere. Leather-sandaled hippies strolled through the town's streets, and the smell of patchouli comingled with the smell of frying tortillas and open sewers.

After inquiring about lodging at various posadas around town, Mom and Dixie settled in at the Quinto Loreto. Every evening in the Quinto's courtyard, a dark-haired man practiced his guitar. Though he looked like a hippie—long-haired, bearded—he wasn't one. He was older, thirty-three, and he didn't like two signature hippie activities: listening to rock 'n' roll or doing drugs. He preferred classical music and weight lifting. They didn't have barbells in Mexico, so most mornings he could be found bench-pressing large rocks in the courtyard. His body was lean and muscular, and he liked feeling strong. His name was George Carpenter. Dad.

One night, fleeing the heat of his room, his shirt off, Dad sat in the courtyard of the Quinto playing a new Spanish song he was trying to master: "Estudious." He held the guitar high and proud; his boot-clad feet tapped out the tempo. As he played, his eyes grew a little teary. Dixie and Mom, wearing peasant skirts and no bras, listened to him play while they smoked cigarettes. When he finished, my mom, long-limbed and blond; and Dixie, dark-haired and worldly, crept closer to him.

The ladies lit up another round. Dad didn't smoke. They talked about their travels. They were headed farther south, probably to the Yucatan. They were letting fate guide them. Mom was waiting for word from various graduate schools. She was almost twenty-seven years old and was feeling the siren call of adventure.

That night in the courtyard Dad told them terrific stories about his travels in France and his new passion: working in the forest. When Dad stood up to tell a story about some Gypsies he met in Europe, he strutted around like a Shakespearean actor, his face animated and flushed. Mom felt herself becoming enchanted. She had never met a man like him before. He could speak French and was well traveled. And he could fell a tree. Her previous boyfriends had been intellectuals with not much life experience. And then there was the music. His love, splayed out for the guitar: that was sexy as hell.

It is a romantic story, and when my mom tells it, she casts the night as a competition between her and Dixie: who would get to claim this handsome guitar player? Knowing that I wouldn't exist if Dad favored Dixie, I always find myself cheering for my mom and her feminine wiles. As it turned out, Dixie gave up first, yawning, and walked back up the stone steps to the room. Dad and Mom's fate—and mine— was sealed. They spent the night together. Soon they were a couple, waving good-bye to Dixie and her VW bus.

The adventures continued: After hitchhiking through Mexico, they returned to the USA and ended up in Crescent, Oregon, where my father had worked for the Forest Service.

There, they lived on the cheap. They rented an A-frame with no plumbing, and my dad returned to his old post, saving up money so they could travel to Europe. In early 1970 they boarded a freighter ship with their newly acquired dog, Zachary, bound for Spain. Mom had been accepted to a graduate program in educational psychology at San Francisco State University, but she opted to travel with Dad instead.

Docking in Alicante, they bought a van and set off to live like Gypsies. They stayed on the island of Formentera and became inspired by the small farms they saw there. After six months of island life, they drove to the South of France, traveling from vineyard to vineyard, picking grapes. Mom was a slow picker, but Dad made up for it—he was tremendously strong, able to pick up crates of grapes without effort. The foremen loved him, this mustachioed American with excellent French. As pickers, they were paid daily with a small sum of money, a loaf of crusty bread, and two bottles of wine. Dad was happy to be back in France, and wanted to stay as long as possible.

But then Mom got word that her mom was dying of bone cancer. She felt horrible, pausing to retch into the vines as she picked. She was pregnant. She flew to Southern California to take care of her mom, while Dad stayed behind to sell the van in Spain before flying back. My grandmother, Mary Virginia, met Riana only as a bump in Mom's belly.

With my mom's inheritance, they began scoping out land to buy. They wanted a big ranch where they could have a farm with cattle. My dad wanted to be far away from town and other neighbors. Headquartered again at the A-frame in Crescent, they looked at properties in Oregon and Idaho before they stumbled across the town of Orofino. The location was ideal, on a big river, and the rolling hills reminded them of Spain. They camped out along the Clearwater, my mom enormously pregnant, until they found the ranch: one hundred and eighty acres for $30,000. The locals thought this was a ludicrously high amount. "Damn city kids," they snorted at the Ponderosa Café when they heard the price. The ranch came with a tattered trailer that Mom set up as their temporary home. They planned to stay there for only a year. By then, they would move into the big house they were going to build from scratch. They earmarked copies of *Sunset* magazine for inspiration. The house was going to be epic.

Inspired by books they had read while traveling, like Helen and Scott Nearing's *The Good Life*, and *Malabar Farm*, my parents set up a chicken coop, a large garden, rabbit hutches. They got married at the Orofino City Hall. My parents believed they would be like Ma and Pa Kettle, sitting on their rocking chairs on the front porch, growing old together.

At first it was all that they had hoped. The ranch was breathtaking with its gently sloping hills and excellent fields for running cattle. The trailer that came along with the acreage was funky, but was actually a step up from how they had been living in Europe. It had a washer and dryer, and an armchair. Mom, nine months pregnant, was thrilled at these luxuries.

In 1971, just as the Woods' roses were in bloom, my sister, Riana, was born. Dad was happy as a lark living off the land, scraping by, playing guitar, and going fishing and duck hunting. Mom was game too, even with a newborn baby. She religiously read *Mother Earth News* while breastfeeding. Her vegetable garden flourished. They bought a milk cow and

Mom churned butter and made cheese while baby Riana napped.

That winter the pump to the water cistern froze while Dad was gone on one of his elk hunting trips with his Crescent, Oregon, buddy John Garrick. Mom was snowed in, without a car, and six-month-old Riana had dreadful diarrhea. It scared Mom. She melted snow, made do. But on that winter day she realized that the simple life, the one she had so idealized before having children, might actually kind of suck.

But Mom was an optimist, and winter passed. When Dad ordered a bunch of ginseng plants that he planned to deposit in the forest, then later dig up and sell for $300 per pound, she smiled and nodded her head. "Cool." While the ginseng grew, in the meantime, in order to buy materials to build their house, Dad took timber thinning jobs. Mom worried when he went out into the forest. She had heard of the dangers of logging, of branches called widow makers, that could fall and crush a man.

In April 1972 Mom discovered she was pregnant again. At first Mom was excited—lots of children were part of their plan. But by summer the washing machine broke and she had to clean Riana's diapers in the bathtub. Her hormones were raging. Dad discovered Mom weeping against the side of the trailer, muttering, "No. No. No," and crying. He urged her to go see her aunt in California. "With what money?" she demanded. "In what car?" He shrugged. They used to be proud to call themselves the voluntary poor. But they needed money to finish building their dream house, to pay for seed, and for vet bills if one of the cattle my dad had insisted on buying got sick.

Mom rallied. She continued farming through her pregnancy. With Riana strapped to her back, she rototilled the vegetable garden and chopped firewood. She even took to strapping a hubcap to her pregnant belly before milking the cow, who was a kicker.

In December I was born, named after Novella Calligaris, an Italian who swam in the 1972 Summer Olympics, winning three medals, including a silver in the women's four-hundred-meter freestyle. Dad began planting Scotch pines. "Christmas trees!" he explained to Mom when she asked where their little savings had gone. He had bought saplings that would become the perfect Yuletide trees. My mom just nodded her head and tightened her lips.

In 1974, on the other side of the Clearwater River from my parents, a commune appeared. It was called Farm Out. Founded by a couple from the east coast, Lowell and Marcia, their goal was self-sufficiency. But unlike Mom and Dad, they weren't on their own. They had friends from Cornell living there, and there were stragglers who showed up and stayed for years. Everyone worked together, and they knew how to party. My mom met them first at the farmer's market in downtown Orofino, where they were selling vegetables, goat cheese, and honey. Lowell was blond and bearded, Marcia had an easy, gap-toothed smile. They were young and cool, and idealistic. Mom was intrigued, and remembered with longing her Berkeley days. Dad scoffed when Mom told him the cheese reminded her of Formentera; he wasn't looking for friends, he preferred to be alone.

It wasn't long before Mom started taking me and Riana up to Farm Out on her own. It was at Farm Out that Mom caught wind of a new-fangled idea: Women's Lib. At Farm Out, men baked bread and mopped floors—and they helped out with child rearing. Try as she might, though, Mom couldn't get my Hemingway-loving father to share in childcare or household chores. Their dream house was not finished. It lumbered off in the distance, just a skeleton next to a stand of old-growth trees. By then they had started calling it the Rough House. Two years on the land, and we still lived in that damn trailer.

Mom began to spend more time at Farm Out, and Dad grew increasingly resentful.

By 1975, we finally moved into the Rough House. It was definitely unfinished and rough, but there was a roof. Then, one day, Dad was gone. I do remember the fight that ended everything. Dad came into the kitchen, tall and raging, and threw a glass of lemonade at my mom's face. She fought him off, and Riana and I defended Mom. Riana grabbed a butter knife and I jumped on my dad's leg. I was so little I only reached up to his cowboy-boot-clad shin. "Leave Mommy alone," we yelled. "We'll kill you if you hurt her," my sister raved. Dad sobbed, kicked us off his legs, and ran out of the house.

He ended up moving to a shack by the Clearwater River. By 1976 the divorce was finalized. Mom finished the Rough House with her old friend Dixie, who had moved to Orofino, and a new boyfriend named Duward who happened to be a carpenter. They ran electricity, nailed sheets of dry wall across the skeleton of wood framing, and hung doors. She salvaged wood from a defunct gymnasium in Orofino and paneled the wall behind the old-fashioned cookstove. Riana and I saw Dad for birthday parties and Christmas. But mostly he was gone, and an uneasiness evaporated. There was no custody battle.

With Dad gone, Farm Out became a bigger part of our lives. We loved Lowell, who reminded us of a bear, and who always gave us honey to eat. We also loved the goats, who looked at us with their weird eyes, flicking their tongues. We became fixtures on the land and at the legendary summer solstice parties. The whole town would show up for these annual parties, toting six-packs of beer, bottles of wine. I remember sitting around the bonfire until it got so hot that everyone, men and women alike, took their shirts off. Joints were passed.

It was at one of these parties that my mom met Tom, a commune member with dark hair and a mellow pot smoker's demeanor. He would become her long-term, but also long-distance, boyfriend.

In 1978, when I was five and Riana seven, we moved to Washington State. Mom got a teaching job there. Mom asked Dad if he cared if we left. He said that he didn't. We met up with Dad one last time at the Ponderosa Café. We had been living in a teepee at my mom's boyfriend Tom's house that summer, shaking earwigs out of our clothes every morning and gazing up at the starry sky at night. Riana and I perched at the sticky counter at the Ponderosa while my mom waited, parked outside in the car, stuff packed for Washington, chain smoking Salems. We didn't know it then, but she was terrified of Dad, what he might do. His tempers were epic.

At the café Dad descended upon us with kisses and hugs, smelling of wood smoke and tree sap, professing his love with a force that scared us. We hadn't seen him much since the divorce, and he was starting to fade from my reality. He ordered us Dr Peppers and burgers. While we ate, he stroked our hair, and seemed to jump out of the stool with his frenetic, cagey energy. Then he was gone, driving a different truck from the last time we saw him. Then it was our turn to disappear.

Feral sisters: Riana and Novella on Hood Canal,
about to go oyster hunting, 1978.

Four

After sending Dad my request to see him, I didn't have to wait long for his reply. The next day he wrote that the huckleberries would be ripe in August, and that would be a good time to visit.

The same day that I got his e-mail, I also got my period. I looked at the blush of blood, like a squashed thimbleberry. For the first time in my life, I regretted getting my period. I didn't know then that this would happen to me nine more times before it was time to set off for Idaho to reunite with my father. Becoming a mother would be more difficult than I had thought.

When I first got his e-mail invitation I was thrilled. I grew dizzy with the things we would do together: We would go foraging! Maybe bow hunting! The missing years would knit together. We could fill each other in on what had happened, what mistakes had been made, and what we had learned from our long absences. I imagined the lost woodlands of my childhood, the lush forest of Idaho, the sleepy town of Orofino with its sweet, clear river.

I could romanticize all this, as I left Idaho, and pretty much my dad, for good when I was five.

When we left, Mom portrayed the move away from Idaho as a big adventure. "There is a big ocean and giant mountains," she told us while she drove away from Orofino headed to Washington State, "and salmon." My sister and I were game. Of the many teaching jobs Mom applied for, she had gotten only one job offer: Hood Canal school, a K–8 on the Skokomish Indian reservation. The rez was on the Olympic Peninsula, on what's often called the wet side of Washington State. Idaho rubs up against Washington's eastern border, which is known as the dry side.

We drove for miles through the Palouse—the golden hills of wheat that roll through Idaho and eastern Washington. Then over the pass that marks the separation of the dry side from the maritime side of Washington State. Our things were packed into milk crates, which rattled against the back windshield. Our two house cats came along with us, panting in fear, crouched under the backseat.

The final miles of the journey brought us to the road to our soon to be home near Union, WA. The road was called the Purdy Cutoff. It was carved out of a lush forest of cedar and Douglas pine, hillsides thick with ferns and the constantly thriving blackberry vines. Even in the height of summer, the hills were blanketed by green moss. The August sun strobed through the leaves and hit the windshield. "It's like *The Hobbit*!" we gasped. Mom's boyfriend Tom told us that we had hobbit feet—tough and calloused from walking around the ranch barefooted. Mom had read us JRR Tolkien's book, priming us for the journey. Tom had left Farm Out by then. He was getting his PhD in soil science at the University of Idaho in Moscow, and so stayed in Idaho with the promise he would eventually join us in Washington.

Our car heaved up on the gravel parking spot next to the cabin, which lay along the shoreline of the Hood Canal. The rental house—our new home—was tiny, painted green; it lay at the foot of some treacherous stairs. There was a small lawn, and a pier with a dock that gently rocked in the briny water. The fine green algae that grew on the dock looked like fairy hair to me, waving in the gentle waves. My sister and I had never tasted salt water before.

Everything was different, compared to Idaho. Instead of morel mushrooms, there were golden chanterelles. These grew on the steep hillside next to the cabin, glowing as they emerged from the moss-covered forest floor. The Clearwater River was replaced by the murky Skokomish River. Instead of the red-winged blackbirds who nested in the duck pond at the ranch, there were seagulls with their yellow beaks and beggar's nature. There weren't soft, dusty thimbleberry bushes, just the aggressive blackberry brambles. Chinook salmon, not rainbow trout, were sold by the Skok tribe, wood-smoked until they were orange and drenched with the taste of alder.

The cabin Mom rented was really meant to be a summer cabin—it had no insulation. But it came with furniture and it was cheap. Her new job was teaching fourth grade. She was thirty-seven and this was her first professional job. She shopped for schoolteacher clothes like corduroy skirts and cardigans and got a perm. Riana and I cried in terror when she came home from the hair salon, her long straight hair gone.

My sister and I dove into the new landscape and searched for what it had to offer. The ocean became our larder. Riana and I walked down the beach, carrying our oyster knife with us. We shucked the oysters right there on the rocky shore, gulping them down, brine and all. Eric, a towheaded kid who lived a few docks down and was as feral as we were—but in a maritime way—recognized us as allies, and taught us some of his tricks. He motored us around the canal in his dingy and showed us how to catch Dungeness crab. The secret was rotten chicken backs. We tossed the rotted flesh into crab pots, sunk the trap into the water, and waited. It took only a few hours before the cage became full of writhing crabs. Eric showed us how to tell which ones were the males by the marks on their bellies, and those were the legal ones to take. We pulled blue-black mussels from the dock pilings and steamed them until their tender orange flesh was revealed.

We weren't living on the ranch anymore, but life was still wild. A few weeks after my sixth birthday I walked down the pier and encountered a sea lion. He had been slumbering peacefully as I approached. He was covered with short brown hair and reeked of salty rot. As I stood next to him he opened his eyes and considered me. We contemplated each other for a while, then I reached out and patted his rump. His fur felt stiff yet soft. He made no move. Mom spotted me from the kitchen and let out a yell. Sea lions are known to be aggressive, knocking people into the water. Gouging them. Not my guy. He gently slipped into the water with a backward look, almost apologetic.

In 1980, Mount Saint Helens erupted. Though the mountain was 140 miles away, plumes of fine gray powder shrouded the sky. The devastation was epic: the blast was four hundred times stronger than the Hiroshima nuclear bomb; one hundred and fifty square miles of old-growth forest were destroyed.

As an eight-year-old, I was hopeful about the blast. Maybe

I wouldn't have to go to school? I dreaded the classroom. One of my grade school teachers wrote the following evaluation about me: "Novella, as you know, is not a normal child, and never will be."

When I was in second grade we moved again. It was so cold in the winter, and the landlords wanted to raise the rent on the cabin. We relocated away from the shores of the Hood Canal and into Shelton, a logging town ten miles from the canal. I learned to replace the beach's larder with Mickey's Deli, just across the alley from our new house. I had never had such immediate and direct access to candy before. I became a regular, slurping up Reese's Peanut Butter Cups instead of oysters. I quickly forgot about wild things. By then, Dad was almost completely forgotten.

Sometimes someone from school would ask "Where's your dad?" knowing it would get a rise out of me. Not having a dad, I sensed, made me different from the other kids. I knew he was a logger—that's what the postcards he had sent said. So I repeated that, saying that he was in a logging camp, and so he couldn't come home, he could only send postcards. Some of the other kids in Shelton (home of the Highclimbers) had logger dads. I studied their dads' clothing: Levi's cut off at the shin, red suspenders, steel-toed boots. I imagined my dad dressed like that too.

I began experiencing pains in my leg. Debilitating pains that kept me home from school, where I would fry bacon and watch *The Young and the Restless*. My mom took me to a doctor and after a session of X-rays and exams, he asked to speak with her alone. I'm pretty sure that's when he told her that I was faking.

My mom, ever resourceful, came up with an idea to get me to go to school: stuffed animals. In addition to several house cats, I had a dizzying array of stuffed animals. What if Novella, she asked my teachers, could bring some of her stuffed animals with her to school? Every day I arrived at Evergreen Elementary with a plush polar bear, or Cookie, my stuffed monkey. They helped me make friends and get through the day.

I distinctly remember one day when, at recess, I deliriously tossed my polar bear into the air, a gang of children surrounding me in awe and delight. I knew in my heart of hearts that the polar bear I held in my arms was not real, not like the sea lion on the dock of the Hood Canal was real. The white plush toy was just a surrogate, an image I could make alive with my imagination. In a similar way, this was how I started to think of my dad. Because he was never around, it became natural to think of him however I wanted. In my mind, I created my perfect dad: friendly, helpful, loving. And best of all, my dad surrogate could shape-shift for my changing needs.

We got along fine without Dad. Mom had a good job and was frugal with money. She also made lots of friends, and started a garden at our new house in town. Tom came to live with us in Shelton every summer, on break from school, giving her a break from being a single parent.

Then, right after she turned forty, Mom woke up one morning to find her left eye had drifted off to one side. She couldn't focus. Doctors didn't know what it was. They told her to wear an eye patch. I didn't understand and it freaked me out. To me, it seemed that Mom had turned into a pirate. She felt exhausted all the time, and needed to take long naps after work. She didn't know it then, but her immune system was attacking the myelin sheaths that lined her nerves. Eventually she was diagnosed with multiple sclerosis.

Instead of drawing our family closer together, Mom's illness allowed me and my sister to run more wild. While my mom napped on the couch, Riana, who was just in middle school, was off smoking pot with high schoolers. I was in fifth grade, stealing money from my mom's wallet to buy more candy. I had a major sugar addiction. I was giddy with the freedom my mom's illness offered. Dad was only in the picture in that he sporadically sent us child support money. I began to value the money more than actually seeing him. I definitely didn't fear any disciplinary action that he, as a father, might have delivered. Except the one time Mom actually used Dad as a form of punishment.

By 1984 Riana and I were both out of control. Riana got busted shoplifting a pair of Guess Jeans. I was twelve and was sure I could get away with anything. Candy no longer held as much of an appeal—I had discovered cigarettes. I would fish cigarette butts out of the ashtray of my mom's Honda Civic (dubbed the rice burner by locals) and smoke them. When I took a hit from the bent cigarette, it tasted like burned mint, then I would feel my brain go frail and empty and almost pass out. It was a fantastic trick.

Then one day I almost burned down an apartment building. My accomplice was my new best friend, a good girl who lived down the street.

My new best friend and I sat on a bare mattress in the middle of an empty apartment that I had found a couple doors down from my house. We were puffing away. I noticed she wasn't inhaling but didn't say anything. I loved going to her house because her mom was a homemaker and would often bake us cakes. Their house had hardwood floors and smelled like Murphy wood soap. Our house, in contrast, had funky blue shag carpet that always smelled of cat pee.

I had filched a pack of matches from my mom's purse and started striking them, watching the flame come and then burn out. After a while, I held one of the matches up to the lacy curtains that hung in the window. The flame surged and bolted up the curtain, disintegrating the whole thing to the rod. "Cool," my new best friend and I giggled. I burned another curtain while she watched.

Some of the unburned curtain fell to the floor and I gathered it into a pile on the mattress. "Watch this," I said. The mattress caught on fire almost immediately, melting the polyester lining and searing a black hole into the middle. We ran. The blaze and smoke alerted the landlord and we were caught. I had to pay for the mattress and curtains, and she and I weren't allowed to play together anymore. My other punishment: Although we had had virtually zero contact with Dad since leaving Idaho, I was sent to live at his house for the summer.

As it happened, Dad was living in the Rough House. After we left Idaho for good, Mom tried to sell her half of the ranch which included the Rough House and ninety acres. No one was willing to buy an unpermitted house in the middle of nowhere. Then Dad offered to buy it. He had reunited with his high school sweetheart, and though he had almost no money of his own, he cajoled her into buying the house and the land.

Dad met up with Mom for the daughter handoff in Yakima. Riana came along with me, and we brought our cats too. Mom went to Tom's house in Moscow that summer; Dad took us back to Orofino, up to the ranch.

It was like we had never left the ranch, everything was the same. We climbed up the wide wooden front porch where Riana and I had learned to pee standing up. I clamped down the front door's black metal latch and swung the door open into the kitchen. The sink was to the right; the woodstove where Mom cooked us pancakes was still there on the left. I scampered down the low-slung set of stairs that led to the living room and felt the cool red clay tiles. The windows, covered in spiderwebs, looked out over the Idaho hills.

Though the house looked the same, Riana and I were very different by then. We had fully embraced the greed-is-good ethos of the 1980s. I watched the television show *Dynasty* and fully related to Krystle Carrington. I was a hick girl in a hick town living in a house that smelled like cat piss, but I liked to imagine myself flying in helicopters and striding through my twenty-three-bedroom mansion. When I got rich (winning the lottery), I wrote in my diary, I would buy "mass clothes" and a mansion for my sister and mom. I also planned to buy a three-story condo in California for my best friends. Dad was not included in the distribution of my fantasy prize winnings.

My sister and I had turned into rabid consumers of trendy garments like Coca-Cola polo shirts and Benetton sweaters. My sister, smelling of Giorgio of Beverly Hills, liked to take a crimping iron to her hair; I rolled mine up in hot rollers and slept on them at night so I would have spiraling princess hair. "The bigger the hair, the closer to god," was the ideal, and hairspray sealed my tidal wave of hair.

When Dad picked us up that summer, who knows what he made of us. Disgust, probably.

The first night back at the Rough House, we sat around the kitchen table eating a pot of Dad's favorite—creamed corn from a can. Dad's girlfriend had thick, wavy blond hair and birdlike features. She seemed annoyed with our presence. Riana and I retold the story of Tom from Farm Out who had cooked a bug on the wood burning stove to illustrate the point that many people in the world eat insects. But he picked a stink bug, and the entire house filled with a bomb of formic acid. Bringing up Tom—my mom's boyfriend—was a bad idea. Dad frowned and got up from the table and threw his bowl into the sink.

"You two, I'm surprised," Dad's girlfriend said in her breathy, halting way that I later learned to associate with new age, crystal-charging people. "You have appalling table manners." Riana and I looked at each other. Instead of using spoons, we had raised the bowls to our lips and were slurping up the creamed corn, dribbling it onto our shirt fronts. Our mom had taught us something she called "Princess Manners" that we were to use in straight society. But being back at the ranch, with just Dad and his girlfriend, we didn't think we should have to use these manners, which we reserved for Thanksgiving and when we went to other people's homes.

Apparently we were wrong: Dad's girlfriend showed us the proper way to dip the spoon in—moving it away from our bodies, then up to our lips. We tried this method for a few bites, then put the spoons down with a clatter and resumed slurping. "Fuck her," said Riana later, and I nodded. I loved the F-word.

Lucky for Dad's girlfriend, she seemed to be getting a John Denver–like rocky mountain high living up on the ranch. She painted frescoes on the walls of the house. Balanced precariously on a ladder, she carefully penciled in sheaves of wheat and grapes onto the upper walls, then painted them with natural colors. She also took long walks on the ranch, communing with nature.

At that time in our lives—I was twelve, Riana fourteen—we snickered at loving nature. We didn't want to rediscover childhood hiding spots or the grove where we found the morel mushrooms. We preferred sitting upstairs, in our old bedroom, listening to a transistor radio and making prank phone calls. "Are you the bird that shit on my window?" we would ask a Bird dialed from the Orofino telephone book. When we got bored of that, we played poker. We used salted peanuts instead of money, which were actually high stakes because there wasn't a lot of food at the Rough House that summer. There was nothing else to do: we were trapped in the middle of nowhere.

As the summer wore on, I missed Mickey's Deli and its cornucopia of candy. Riana wrote long letters to her older boyfriend. We attempted to smoke hay, but it just wasn't the same as my mom's cigarette butts. My dad's girlfriend, if she had a stash of marijuana, kept it well-hidden.

Dad was never there during the day; we never asked where he went. He appeared toward evening, and we were vaguely scared of him, of his intensity, when he asked what we had been doing. If Dad's girlfriend didn't cook a meal, he would fix us something strange like cucumber salad with mayonnaise, black pepper, and chunks of deer jerky. The gamey fat from the jerky coated the roof of my mouth and left a wild taste on my tongue.

I kept a journal that summer my sister and I were sent to Dad's. My mom had given me a small green diary with a lock and key. About the ranch, I described a day when Dad had us help a neighbor bale hay as "sucking." My arms grew welts from touching the rough hay bales, and we were covered with dust by the end of the day. Afterward we went swimming at Zan's Beach on the Clearwater. My dad went in naked as we changed into our suits in the cab of the truck, embarrassed about our changing bodies.

That summer I clandestinely read my sister's journal. One entry haunted me; she wrote, "You hear that girls look for a man who is like their father. Since I don't see my father or write to him that often, I don't know what he 'is like' but I know how my mother is, she has been both parents to me." I hadn't heard this concept of girls looking for a man like their father. Maybe, I thought with horror, as I closed her diary, I will never have a boyfriend because of my missing dad.

When my sister and I returned home from Idaho, back to our mother, we rejoiced at her stable schedule and regular meals. If we misbehaved, she would threaten: "Do you want to go stay with your dad again?" We did not.

Twenty-five years had passed since punishment summer, and now I would be going back to Orofino. Of course I was an adult, now poised to become a parent myself, but the thought of returning to Orofino made me feel like a twelve-year-old again, filled with dread at the prospect of long days spent with a man I barely knew. As the months counted down, I started to feel a quiver of what can only be described as fear. Returning to Orofino was not going to be an easy journey.

PART II

—

RETURN

John Garrick and Dad with an eight-point buck head
mounted on the pickup.

Five

In August, ten months after Dad had gone missing, Bill and I packed the least of our destroyed cars and prepared to drive north, to visit my dad in Orofino. Our steed for the trip was Rosie, a vegetable oil–powered diesel Mercedes, painted red. Someone had given Bill the car, and for some reason it always had a fine dusting of vegetable oil particles on the *inside* of the windshield. But no matter, it ran tolerably well, even though when going up hills the tires sent out a horrible odor.

Before we left I lovingly watered our garden. It was lush with beds of multicolored lettuce and vining green beans. The tomatoes were just starting to blush red. We had been farming on the abandoned lot next to our apartment for years. We never asked permission, we just starting growing food and no one had stopped us. Now that I looked back on it, the whole farming enterprise might have been inspired by my mom and her green thumb. She always had a garden, even post–Rough

House. Though I was a grudging weeder during my youth and spent most of my twenties actively avoiding any kind of vegetable production, it must have trickled in, only to seep out later.

We left the farm under the care of a dependable sitter; it would have to continue without me for the next three weeks. Mostly I was worried about the farm animals. When I checked on the rabbits, a senior rabbit doe named Sasquatch was making plans to give birth. I put a nesting box in her cage and she feverishly began gathering straw and pulling out fur from her chest to make a nest for the new babies.

I walked out into the backyard to say good-bye to the goats. My favorite doe, Bebe, was thick with gestating goat kids. I had bred her to a little chamois named Beach Bum— his mother had a tremendous udder that I was hoping would get passed on to Bebe's kids. She scrambled to her feet in order to give me a nuzzle. I scratched under her neck. "Bitch," I whispered, jealous of her pregnant belly.

Goats made breeding seem so easy. Why weren't my eggs getting fertilized? Nine months since we had started trying, Bill and I were still not pregnant. I had started tracking my temperature and monitoring mucous levels.

It was an odd position to be in, this desperation to get knocked up. Bill and I had always pledged we would never have children. *Breeders*, we used to scoff when we spotted a stroller-pushing couple. *Another life ruined*, I would sigh when I saw a woman cradling a chubby baby.

Instead of breeding baby humans, Bill and I had bred other animals—rabbits and ducks and chickens. In 2008 we started raising Nigerian Dwarf goats. I started with a pregnant Bebe, who dropped two kids in February. By the summer I had weaned them and began milking her. I transformed the surplus milk to make excellent yogurt and a variety of cheeses. These kids, I remember thinking as I watched their springy antics, were way better than human babies. No diapers, no sleepless nights. They slept in the shed in the backyard and didn't cramp my social life.

But a year later, during the spring kidding season, my brain shifted. After helping Bebe deliver another one of her kids, I watched the new goatling suckle, milk gathering at the corner of its mouth. Bebe licked the kid's bottom as it nursed. The new little goat filled me with love, as usual. But it also filled me with something new: longing. The birth had been intensely beautiful. A thought occurred to me: *I could do that too.*

Once the baby-making idea was implanted, my brain would not let go. I started having a recurring dream where I caught a baby falling from the sky; that my breasts had turned into a goat's udder. At book stores, while Bill perused the travel books, I slipped into the birth/pregnancy section to secretly devour books like *A Child Is Born,* marveling at the process of human gestation and birthing. In this book I saw an electron microscope image of women's ovaries, arranged chronologically. The ovaries of a woman in her early twenties were soft and ripe, fertile; but as they aged, getting closer to my age, they hardened, cracked. *Are these my ovaries?* I wondered, looking at the wizened reproductive organs. Time was running out.

Feeling like I probably only had five viable eggs left, I revealed my horrible secret to Bill. After some negotiation, we jumped in the sack, and breeding a human became our goal. In my fever to reproduce, all my reasons for not wanting children—financial worries, loss of freedom—fell away.

As I kissed my goat Bebe good-bye, I remembered one

key thing I had learned from goat breeding: lines are everything. This nugget would also apply to Bill and my offspring,
of course. Bill's stock was West Virginia farm kids on his
mom's side, sturdy religious Midwesterners on his father's
side. My mom was all southern California wholesomeness.
My dad, though, was a blank, uncharted. We climbed into
the car, and I realized that, in a few days, I was about to enter
that uncharted territory with new eyes, and new questions.

We drove up I-5, then forked east into Central Oregon, my
dad's old stomping grounds. In Oregon we took a pit stop in
Crescent. I wanted to meet John Garrick, my dad's hunting
buddy from back in the day. When Dad and I had spent time
together in Idaho Falls, my dad had told me about meeting
John, and how he had changed his life.

In the spring of 1961, while still enrolled at Berkeley, Dad
had written a letter to the Deschutes National Forest inquiring about a summer job. That part of Oregon held a fascination for him. It was vast, vacant, and still seemed wild, unlike
the areas closer to the coast. The Forest Service wrote back:
They had an opening for a young buck surveying timber.
Hard work, low pay. Thrilled, once classes let out in June, he
climbed onto his black motorcycle, pointed it north, and rode
to Central Oregon. At a gas station in Crescent he stopped for
fuel and struck up a conversation with the owner, Mr. Garrick. "I'm looking for a place to stay," he told him. George's
skin was already dark tan, his hair was long, he wore a black
leather motorcycle jacket.

"Mr. Garrick thought I was a beatnik," my dad had said,
and smiled. "He rented me a one-room cabin." The next week,
my dad reported for duty at the Forest Service. His job, he

was astonished to hear, was to walk through the forest all day and look for sick trees. "I couldn't believe we were getting paid to do that," he said. He walked fifteen miles a day, scrambling up hillsides. It was nothing to him. At night, he frequented the local café, the Mohawk. A man named Blacky owned the place, his wife was Belgian and spoke French, so Dad could practice his favorite language. Blacky and Helen loaned him $200 to buy his first chainsaw, and he learned how to fell a tree.

"That was the summer I met John Garrick," he told me as we ate our beans and rice in my Idaho Falls apartment. John—the son of the gas station owner in Crescent. "God, what a wonderful man." John was short, stocky, and quiet; he had been a hunter his whole life. Even though his summer job was up, Dad stuck around because he wanted to learn, from John, how to hunt for elk.

"One night, I spent the whole damn night crouched on a trail, waiting for a deer to walk by," my dad said. "Had my bow and arrow stretched out. Read about that at the library." John knew that wouldn't work. He took my dad to the spots in the forest where he knew the elk frequented. He showed him how to track wildlife, how to be silent in the woods, to wait. John promised they would bag an elk together, and they did. That fall Dad went back to college, but after he dropped out he returned to Crescent to learn more about the forest from John.

"Heck of a guy, god almighty," my dad had said.

John was almost like a mythological creature to me. I was anxious to meet an actual friend of my dad's. John still lived in Crescent. We pulled off the highway there and saw that the Mohawk Café—where my dad hung out back in the early 1960s—was still there. It had an antique neon sign and a blue tiled roof. It was dim inside, and the walls were lined with taxidermied animals, including twenty-one baby fawns, which are disturbingly embryonic looking. We settled into a back table and ordered eggs and hash browns. I noticed the chandelier—which looked like it was made out of rawhide—started swinging on the ceiling for no reason at all.

"Is Blacky here?" I asked the waitress as she filled my cup with ice water.

"Who, honey?" she said. I explained he maybe used to be the owner.

"I don't know anything about that," she said, and wandered off to fill up other customers' coffees. I don't know why I thought Blacky would still be around, but I looked longingly at the bar, imagining my father hunched over it, speaking French.

"OK, I'll call John," I said, getting out my cell phone, suddenly panicked that I wouldn't get to see him.

His wife answered, and after I explained I was George Carpenter's daughter, she invited us to come by. John lived a few blocks from the café.

When we drove up, John opened the door to his house with a grin. He was wearing thick glasses and a camo baseball hat; a pair of black suspenders held up his pants. I liked him immediately.

He had built his house, he explained as we settled on the couch. Including the giant river-rock fireplace that we sat by in the living room, rock by rock.

"So you're looking for your dad?" He smiled.

I nodded. "We're going to go fishing or hunting maybe," I said.

"Your dad was a real honest-to-goodness mountain man," John said. "I remember one time, your dad and I were planning an elk hunting trip, and we weren't sure if we were going to go north or south, along the lake or up in the mountains . . ." I settled back in the couch, soaking up his story. "We were getting ready to really rough it, to go way out. I drove up along that windy road to your parents' property, and when I got there your dad was all flustered," John said.

"He said, 'you weren't blowing an elk bugle were you?' 'No,' I said, 'why?' 'Are you sure? You aren't pulling my leg?'" John chuckled. And then he heard it: an elk bugling right there on the property of my parents. They only had to hike a mile or two into the woods on the ranch before they encountered, and shot, an eight-point buck. "We didn't need to drive anywhere to go hunting—that buck was right there."

"Do you still hunt?" I asked, hungry for more stories about hunting. In preparation to see Dad, I had attended a primitive skills camp where I learned to stalk wildlife and throw a Native American hunting tool called the atlatl. I was sure this was going to impress my dad, especially when we went out into the forest together.

"Nope," John grinned. "Hon, get me my photos," he told his wife.

She bustled into a back room and came back with some printouts. Blurry photos of deer and one of a bobcat. John explained: instead of hunting, he sets up cameras in the woods and takes photos of the wildlife.

"Have you seen my dad lately?" I asked, trying not to look disappointed that he was no longer the great hunter, the hero of my dad's stories.

"It's been five or six years," John said. Maybe he sensed my disappointment. "There was a time once when I really made your dad angry," John said gently.

"Yeah?" I said.

"We were out hunting, out at the swamp. And I was in the truck, getting something. Your dad had his rifle, and was standing in the road when who came by but an enormous elk," John said.

"'George,' I whispered. And he saw it. He raised his rifle, and held it there. Just held it! The elk caught the scent of us a second later and was gone." John smiled. "When he got back into the truck, I gave him a bunch of shit, made fun of his manhood, laughed at him," John said. "And I tell you, he gave me this look, and didn't say another word to me the rest of the day, and then I didn't see him for a couple of years."

"What happened?" I asked.

"I don't know what passed with him," John said. "But a few years later we saw each other and were friends again."

"Now you don't hunt," I said.

"Yeah, and you might think I'm a big softie for that," John said. "But I listen to my heart, and I know what's right."

John seemed mildly worried that so much time had passed since he'd last seen my dad—that seemed to be their pattern. Then he took us for a tour and showed us a canoe my dad had built in 1965. John still had it in his garage; it was broken and he was waiting for my dad to come back and fix it.

"How's your mother?" John asked after a while.

"Good, good," I said.

"My god, she was a good-looking woman," he said. I smiled. "They lived in an A-frame just down the road," John said and pointed. They had lived in Crescent while they saved up money before going to Europe, then returned when they were scouting out land to buy with my mom's inheritance.

"Is it still there?" I asked.

"Oh, yeah. In fact, it's for rent!" I smiled. "Your mom was a bit of a Gypsy," John commented. "Like there was no running water, no toilet, but she was fine with that. She went with the flow. I have no idea what she did all day in that A-frame." Sewed baby clothes and read Dr. Spock, from what she told me.

Then there was nothing more to say. I felt awkward, but also needy. I stared at the broken canoe and wanted John to tell me something about my dad that I had never known. But I couldn't think of any other questions, and we had a long drive ahead of us.

We arrived in Orofino the next afternoon. The hills above the green-blue river were gold and bright, marked with gray rock outcroppings and deep green trees. Memories of the river, the land, the little town I carry with me, everything set in amber light, flooded back to me.

The bridge that led from the highway to the village of Orofino had changed. When I was a kid it had been a rickety but ornate metal bridge lit up by a gaudy neon sign advertising the Konkolville Motel. Now it was just a plain slab of concrete. The neon sign had disappeared. Paranoid locals told me that they had moved the metal bridge to make it easier for the government to drive a tank across the river and into town.

After we crossed the river to the right was the public park where Marcia and Lowell from Farm Out used to sell their produce. I had remembered the park as massive, but now it looked scruffy and small, with only enough room for a couple of picnic tables and a baseball diamond. Driving through downtown, I was pleased to see that the Ponderosa Café, where we met up with Dad that last time, was still intact, all paneled walls and comfy booths. The town had a down-and-out feeling to it, chipped paint and overgrown lawns. One house had a sign out front that read: "I need work, will do anything," with a phone number. A drugstore had Orofino High School merchandise for sale—the Orofino Maniacs. The high school used to abut an insane asylum; hence the wild-haired, straitjacket-wearing mascot.

As we cruised through Orofino, I remembered that my dad's birthday had been in mid-June, and I hadn't sent him a card or even an e-mail. He had turned seventy-four. I tried to envision what would happen when we were reunited. Would he be glad to see me? Or would he make an excuse not to spend time with me, like he had with my sister? If I was honest with myself, I was filled with dread at seeing him—and simultaneously I was filled with dread at being rejected by him.

In Orofino the local IGA supermarket is like the zocalo in Mexican towns. It's where everyone gathers, it's the place to be seen. Bill and I made our way there instinctively. There used to be a mechanical pony outside the IGA. My sister and I would sit on it while my parents bought supplies. When someone walked by, we'd ask, "Can we have a quarter?" Rarely would people oblige us—two raggedly dressed towheads—but when they did, the cold steel would be called into action, lightly jostling us for a few minutes of bliss.

The pony was gone and the whole building looked kind of snazzy, like it had been updated in the 1990s. I went inside. I didn't have my dad's phone number—I had forgotten to save the number the police department had given me in October. I went to the photo department to ask for a phonebook.

"There's one somewhere around here," the clerk said and bent down to open a cabinet door. I heard rustling. I stared at the magazine racks, which were so differently stocked than those in the Bay Area. *Hunting and Fishing, Guns and Ammo, Deerkiller.*

"I got one that's ten years old," the mustachioed clerk reported. He slapped a tiny booklet the size of a *Reader's Digest* on the counter. "But nothing changes here anyway."

I raised an eyebrow—that couldn't be right. But I thumbed through the tiny phone book to Carpenter, found George, dialed the number on my cell phone, and then we were talking.

"Hey, Dad," I said, "I'm at the IGA."

"Well, I'll be goddamned!" he yelled. He sounded genuinely surprised, like we hadn't been planning this for months. "I'll be right there," he said. "I live sixteen miles from town."

I went back outside to reorganize our mangled car. Before we left, Rosie the car had been packed in an orderly way. Prepared for outdoor adventures with my dad, I had packed sleeping bags, hiking boots, a water filter, a backpack, and—a last-minute purchase from REI—a tent. After only a few days on the road, the neatly packed car was a shit storm of banana peels, unstuffed sleeping bags, and empty gallon jugs of water. Typical. Bill and I have driven across the United States four times, and taken innumerable longer side trips to places like Baja and Canada, and entropy always gets the best of us.

Then Bill and I sat outside and leaned up against the concrete wall of the store, near the Blue Rhino propane tanks. It was hot and dry. I noticed a water spigot next to where we were sitting and idly turned it on. Water gushed out. I don't know why it surprised me that water came out except that in Oakland these spigots wouldn't work—they were locked to keep strangers from stealing water. I grabbed one of our empty jugs of water and refilled it. I tasted the water—it was crisp, sweet Idaho water. I filled all three of our empty jugs.

Then I saw an old guy over on the other side of the building doing the same thing. As he filled the containers, he was scanning the parking lot.

It was my dad.

"Dad," I called. My heart was beating hard and I felt a little nauseous. He didn't hear me. I walked toward him, suddenly self-conscious. My hair was short and punky, standing up on all ends as it does after a few days of driving. I was wearing my black cowboy boots and Levi's—standard dress code for me—but it suddenly seemed too masculine.

I hadn't seen my dad since our fly-fishing trip four years before. He was wearing black jeans with cowboy boots and a tucked-in, dark blue polo shirt. A baseball hat. He looked even skinnier than last time. He was rummaging in the back of his truck as I approached, then he saw me. "Kiddo!!" He let out a whistle and we hugged.

"You've gotten taller or I've gotten shorter," he said. We were the same height—five eight—but I know he had been taller, at least five eleven. Age shrinks you. But his arms were muscular. Bill stood behind me. "Hey, guy," Dad said and they shook hands.

"Are you hungry?" he asked us and we shook our heads no.

"OK, well, let me get some more water and then we'll go up to my place."

He reached into the back of the truck and pulled out the rest of his empty water bottles. The plastic jugs were so old they had long ago lost their labels and had turned a yellowish color. There were twelve or more so it took a while. I noticed that he tossed them carelessly into the truck bed, so the water jugs went sailing into the air and landed on chunks of wood bark, near a big orange chainsaw.

"I don't have water at my place," he explained. I wasn't surprised—I had imagined that his cabin was off the grid. While using this term does sound cool, the reality of it means filling water jugs at IGA. While he filled jugs, I expected someone to come out and yell at us but no one did.

"Follow my truck?" Dad said.

"Bill, you follow, I'm going to ride with Dad," I said.

I climbed into the truck. The cab was scattered with candy bar wrappers and two shotguns, haphazardly arranged. It reminded me of the trashed car I drove during my summer reporting in Idaho Falls. With that car, you had to open the door with a screwdriver. The passenger seat was always cluttered with water bottles and apple cores.

I kicked a gun out of the way and sat down on the cratered truck seat that was missing a whole section of foam. My butt dipped in at an awkward angle, but I felt right at home in this discomfort. Like father, like daughter.

Mountain man: Dad tanning a deer hide on the ranch, hounds looking on. The town of Orofino in the distance below, 1973.

Six

Dad pulled his truck out of the IGA parking lot and cruised past Main Street to give me the "ten-cent tour." Downtown Orofino looked like the old western town that it was. There was a real estate office housed in an old brick building, the Ponderosa Café, the neon sign for the Clearwater Club Bar. "I play pool there," Dad said, pointing at the bar. *Ah, yes, in the morning,* I remembered the cop describing his daily routine.

Then we drove out of town, winding through a road dotted with houses and trees. After passing an old railroad trestle, it became sparsely populated, thick with trees. Dad whistled while he drove. I rolled down the window and tried not to think about whether the guns next to me were loaded. After ten miles or so, Dad pointed at a sign on the road. "Grangemont Road," he said. Later I found out locals called the area "Strangemont." Then we turned onto Rudo Road, which I recognized from the police report. Making sure he was following, I looked back at Bill driving Rosie and waved. He waved back. Rudo Road was narrow, dense with trees along both sides. After a few miles of this forested road, we pulled into Dad's steep gravel driveway.

The air was cold for August. Must have been the forest, which soared around us, smelling piney. Bill pulled up behind us, the wheels crunching in the gravel. From the outside, Dad's cabin looked rustic. It was a wooden structure covered with cedar shakes. A drying shed off to the side of the driveway was filled with stacks of firewood. I surveyed the place, greedy for every detail, but I felt a little queasy too. There was a pelt of some animal hanging from a post on the drying shed. A beaver? A small bear? I couldn't tell.

"How many cords do you think are in there?" my dad asked me when we got out of the truck. He pointed at the stacks of wood.

"Um . . ." I started. I knew a cord was a unit of measurement. "Five?" I hazarded.

"No, no: eighteen!" he said. "Sold nine of 'em already." He was in great shape, I noticed. Chopping wood for a living.

Then I walked into my dad's house for the first time ever, Dad leading the way, Bill following me. The front stairs into the cabin were a genuine hazard. They slouched to the left and were battered, collapsed, decomposing. In a strange hall-like room were enormous slabs of wood that I would later learn my dad was hoarding to make guitars. There was a terrible smell there in the corridor, so bad even Bill, man immune to noxious odors, covered up his nose. It was as if a skunk had gone into the slabs of wood to die and then slowly oozed out one last stink bomb.

At the sliding door that led into Dad's cabin proper, my

heart sank. We stepped into a dark and shabby living room. Along one wall was a ratty couch with a sleeping bag rolled out on it. In the corner of the room was a woodstove, the chimney askew. His guitar was sitting out near some sheet music next to a frayed chair near the window. Weight lifting barbells lay on the scruffy particleboard floor. Dad was asking about our drive, and I made small talk, but I was taking it all in. The kitchen, off to the left, was narrow like a ship's galley. It was a disaster. Bottles of pills lined the sink, jugs of water were wedged into the sink. Boxes of store-bought cookies lay open on the counter. There were cupboards, but nothing was put away, so the counters were lined with dishes and cups, cans of this and that. On the refrigerator I noticed my name and e-mail address under an "In Case of Emergency" note. Behind the kitchen was a back room. It seemed to be devoted to plastic bags, which were clustered on the floor, hundreds of them, making a giant plastic bag nest. There was no real bathroom—the outhouse was off to the side of the house. I later visited it. It was a bad scene, full to the brim.

"Who built this cabin?" Bill asked.

"Some cowboys," Dad said, but didn't elaborate. "Otto said there would be water," Dad said, talking about the guy who he bought the cabin from thirteen years ago. "But he never did it." That explained why he had to get water at the spigot from IGA.

My eyes scanned the walls. They weren't covered with trophy animals or meaningful pieces of nature like *Pan* but with newspaper clippings and a couple paper printout photos of me and my sister. The clippings were an odd assortment—a photo of a high school girl with an elk she killed with a crossbow, a wedding announcement for a local couple. Tacked on the wall, I noticed a card I had sent to my dad from college; I wanted to read it but was afraid to touch his things.

From the family lore I had been collecting and from my experiences with him fly-fishing that one summer, I expected his cabin to exude rustic charm. Maybe he would have a taxidermied bear in a growling stance next to the fireplace? Crossbows lining the walls. Feathers and bird wings. This was not anything like Glahn's cabin, the cabin I had been imagining him living in for all these years. He had bought this cabin thirteen years ago yet it looked like he just moved in. It wasn't a home so much as it was a den.

There was a flight of stairs in the cabin that led to two upstairs bedrooms, but my dad confessed that he never went up there. The local wildlife—opossums, raccoons, squirrels, bats—had taken over these rooms. After seeing the cabin, Bill and I insisted that we would be very—very—comfortable sleeping in our tent outside.

Dad helped us set up our tent underneath a giant tree. I couldn't find the tent poles and stakes anywhere in the back of our car. "Here ya go," he said when he saw the problem, and, taking a line of rope, strung it through the tent's pole openings until it was tenuously set up. Tying the sides of the tent to nearby tree branches opened up the floor of the tent. Then Dad ran off to the wood-drying area to hone some wooden stakes that he pounded into the ground with a rock. Set up in this fashion, our tent looked like a hobo satellite of my dad's dilapidated cabin. Bill and I threw our sleeping pads and bags into the tent, then joined Dad for dinner.

After our initial catching up, Dad went on a monologue about his life, retelling stories about his time in France, the episode in Spain when he and Mom had bought the van. All territory that we had covered in previous encounters. Bill, bored, yawned and retired to our tent. It was getting late. Then the conversation steered toward the bizarre.

"Now, I've been taught how to kill—how to kill with my bare hands," he started. My ears perked up—is this where we start talking about stalking wildlife? And make plans for going fishing?

"One time these two cops pulled me over," Dad said. "Really, just harassing me. And as I stood there"—he sprang up from the hard chair he was sitting on; I was sitting on the couch where he set up his sleeping bag—"and I thought, OK, how'm I going to kill this one who was standing there—" He pointed across the room. "I could've done a judo chop but then his partner would've shot me." The other time, he told me, was in San Mateo, CA. . . .

As he spoke, animated, and clearly glad to have a pair of attentive ears, I got a horrible sinking feeling. Dad was crazy. He went on a twenty-minute rant about how the police were always bothering him. He looked at me in the middle of the rant, and realizing it was me, his daughter, he customized the story. Washington State cops: They were why he never came to visit me and my sister. Why he missed our graduations and State tennis matches.

He seemed to be getting really agitated. I wanted to calm him, and didn't want him to know that I thought he sounded insane.

"Hmmm. Yes. Cops. Hmmm," I said, glancing at the door. Could I just bolt? "Well Pops, it's been a long day. A long day." And with that I stumbled off to find Bill.

He was in the tent munching on a banana and reading a book about a man with no legs who motorcycled around Siberia.

"How's it going?" Bill asked.

I started to tell him that my dad was acting really weird but Bill has a hearing loss so I had to shout into his ear. I peeked out the tent door. The light was still on in my Dad's cabin and I could see him moving around, still agitated. I felt a little scared. "Let's go to the car," I said. We crept into the car so our voices wouldn't carry.

"Things are not going well," I said, and sighed. "Look at this shit hole! But that's not the problem."

"What's wrong?" Bill asked.

"I think my dad is crazy," I said.

"Think?" Bill said, and laughed. "Why don't we just leave tomorrow?" His voice broke a little.

"What's wrong?" I asked, sitting straight up.

"Nothing," he said.

"Oh, I thought you were going to cry," I said.

"No, I was just burping."

OK, I thought, only Dad is losing it. After the update, Bill and I wandered back out to our tent in the field to go to sleep. I still was holding out hope that Dad and I would go fishing together, and this would pull him out of crazy mode. Maybe it would take him a little time to adjust to having guests, and then we could re-create our time spent fly-fishing in Idaho Falls. Once we were both feeling relaxed, I could reveal to him my plan to get pregnant, find out a little more family history—to really connect.

At daybreak, I awoke and lay in my sleeping bag feeling sorry for myself. Then I heard the sound of a gun firing. I thought it might be my dad, getting ready to give me some shooting lessons. I hurriedly dressed, suddenly filled with hope again.

"Novella!" my dad called from the porch with a touch of hysteria to his voice, "Riana's on the phone!" The shooter turned out to be a neighbor who'd set up a target range on his property and liked to begin his day with a practice session.

I trudged up the jankity stairs and my dad handed me the rotary phone to talk to my sister.

"How's Idaho?" Riana asked.

"Beautiful."

"Are you staying in the cabin—what's it like?" she asked.

"Weird," I whispered, watching Dad out on the porch. I'd have to wait and tell her the full story later. He got out his guitar and started playing a classical version of the Beatles' song "Yesterday" on the porch. He was all atwitter with excitement but couldn't seem to channel it toward us. It was the first time I had heard him play in years—the notes sounded clear and hopeful.

"Did you go up to the ranch?" Riana asked.

"Not yet," I said. "Today."

It would be my first time back at the ranch since Riana and I visited together in 1990. Riana had been in her second year of college then, and I was a high school senior. Riana had stopped smoking pot, and had become interested in physics and chemistry. I'd straightened up too; sports had distracted me from my tendency toward drinking and smoking. I was the captain of the tennis team. We drove Riana's Datsun 510 back across Washington State and into Idaho, planning to meet up with Dad.

By then we had long forgotten the awkwardness of punishment summer, and despite the fact that he had missed my sister's high school graduation, we were excited to see him. Riana was eager to tell him about her impressions of college; I wanted to show him that I was almost an adult. We both hoped the visit would start a new phase of our relationship. But when we got closer to Orofino and called him, he canceled, telling us he was too sick to have visitors, even his daughters.

Disappointed, we decided we would go up to the ranch—we're so close, why not? We hadn't seen the place since 1984. By 1988, Dad's girlfriend broke up with him and he lost the property with the house on it—again. It reverted back to Mom, who let Dad stay there until she could find a new buyer, which she did in 1990.

Back then, the road up to the ranch was as I remembered it—lined with thimbleberries, potholed, wild. We passed the duck pond and the trailer where we had lived and squealed in recognition. But something was wrong: the Rough House was not there, lumbering in the distance. We drove up to the site and saw a pile of burned beams, the golden grass scarred black. We heard the story of the fire later: The new owner had only lived in the house a few weeks before one night he fell asleep with a cigarette in his hand. The place had gone up like a tinderbox. The cedar shakes, the old gymnasium floor walls, all that work, destroyed.

My sister and I sifted around the rubble, looking for artifacts from our childhood, but came up with nothing. I was devastated. My mom portrayed our time on the ranch as our good years, when we had been an intact family—it was only later that I pieced together their hardship. The place was utterly gone. I felt like I had been robbed of a special childhood toy. I longed for Mom to be there with us, to witness the destruction, to buffer me against the harsh realities that later I would learn are part of being alive.

After sifting around the land for a while, we drove away from the ruins of the ranch and eased our pain by smoking clove cigarettes and listening to the Cure's *The Head on the Door* on the long drive back.

Back then I had blamed Dad for the destruction, that he had let that happen to the ranch. I felt disgusted. I started to keep score after seeing the destruction of the Rough House. A few months later, Dad failed to pay Riana's tuition as he had promised, and so she had started taking out student loans and working full-time. Another promise broken.

After talking to Riana on Dad's phone, I hung up and told Dad that I wanted to go out and see the old ranch property again. He handed me a coffee, ready to make a plan for the day. Bill wandered in and sat on the chair.

"Oh, babes," Dad said, "I can't go up there."

"Why not?" I asked.

"That property is possessed," he declared.

Bill and I looked at each other. Oh, no, I thought. I didn't want to hear more, but Dad launched in on a winding narrative of how he had seen Satan up there. Satan resembled a giant chipmunk with slanty goat eyes, he told us. And this giant chipmunk lived up there, haunting the place, making it unlivable for anyone who dared. He listed all the people who had lived on the property—and been cursed with divorce, fire, and death.

In the end, he compromised by agreeing to go see old Max. Dad had gotten ninety acres of the ranch after the divorce. But what with it being haunted, he sold this half of the ranch to Max. Max had built a cabin, which lay right at the edge of the property line of the old ranch.

Dad, Bill, and I drove up the Gilbert Grade and followed the road to the ranch. Max was waiting for us. He turned out to be a sweet man of eighty-four. He tottered outside his hand-hewn cabin built onto a bluff overlooking the field my dad used to plant with alfalfa for the cattle back in his ranching days.

"George," he called out warmly, as we walked up the hill to his house.

"This is my daughter, Novella," Dad said proudly. Max and I shook hands.

Max was withered and slender but he was spry. He had an enormous vegetable garden, which was spilling over with red raspberries, carrots, strawberries.

"You tilled the alfalfa field," my dad said, pointing.

I could tell Dad was having a hard time being there. He seemed uneasy, a little out of breath. Later he told me Max might have some special powers that thwarted the evil spirits that he knew lived on the ranch. I had known my dad was eccentric, but not this kind of eccentric.

"Yep," Max drawled. "Gonna plant me a peach orchard out there." Peaches. My mom had thought she would grow peaches on the ranch too. But according to her it was too cold; the peach trees she planted had died. Forty years later, what with global climate change, maybe those peaches would be possible. The field is a two-acre, circular expanse, and would hold about two hundred trees. I marveled at Max's optimism. If he was very lucky, he'd harvest his first real crop at the age of ninety-two.

Max beckoned us to walk up the ridge with him. We wandered farther up a bluff that was filled with pine trees.

"Wow, this field is growing back," Dad gasped. There were quite a few large-sized pine trees. He had logged this property twenty years ago. My mom had complained that he had cut down most of the trees on the ranch.

"Yep, and a dead one," Max said and pointed at one that had gone red in the needles. I was out of breath from the steep climb up the hill and marveled that old Max had made it at all. In fact, he seemed unfazed. Maybe he did have special powers.

"Want me to take care of that for ya?" my dad asked.

"Oh, sure," Max said.

And then Dad flashed into action. He ran down the rocky hill, jumped in his truck, and spun wheels getting up to where we were. He pulled the orange chainsaw out of the truck bed, strapped on a pair of earmuffs, and stepped toward the dead tree. The chainsaw gunned to life and the faint smell of gasoline drifted toward us. For a few minutes he worked on one side of the tree, wood chips flying, then he made some cuts on the back. The tree, maybe twenty feet tall, crashed and splintered to the ground. It was dry and landed with a soft hushing, not a thud like I had expected. Then my dad jumped on top of the fallen tree like it was a balance beam. Crouched down, he lightly touched the bottom branches of the tree with the chainsaw, then moved up to the next branches and the next until they were all removed. Then he cut the trunk into big chunks, starting at the top, and making five incisions. The tree lay there, dissected.

When he finished felling Max's tree, Dad clambered back toward us and onto the road, dusting chips of wood off his shirt. I was glad to get a glimpse of him doing his work—a mini take-your-daughter-to-work day. Watching him work had reminded me of a story my mom's Farm Out friend Phil told me about my dad. It was the early eighties and Phil had wandered into the local dive bar, the Clearwater Club, where he saw my dad seated at the bar, bleeding profusely from a giant cut in his leg.

"'George, you ought to have someone look at that,'" Phil remarked after ordering a beer.

"'Nope, gotta finish this job—I'm way behind and if I don't come in on time, I don't get paid,'" Dad told him. Phil offered to help. The next day they drove out to the site together. It was a hot summer that year, even in the thick of the forest. The task was to mitigate forest fire by clearing out brush and lumber left over from a big logging company's recent clear-cut. Dad set to work clearing brush, and working at a speed that Phil, a seasoned logger himself, found alarming. "He was like a force of nature," Phil told me, "branches were flying everywhere, his chainsaw moved so fast it was scary. He was like a man possessed. And that was on an injured leg." Phil refused to help the next day—too dangerous—but my dad did manage to get the job done in time and got paid.

Now that I had seen him in action, it dawned on me how dangerous the work he did actually was. Maybe that was why the Orofino police had staged a manhunt, thinking he was dead or injured from his work in the woods. Even felling this small tree on Max's property took an enormous amount of skill and care, and some level of recklessness too.

I looked at the trees around us. I usually look at trees like a goat would—scanning for low, edible branches. But now I could see how Dad saw them. How many cords of firewood a tree would make, how it was leaning, which way it'd fall if you took a chainsaw to it. I wanted to learn something from my dad, to make up for our lost years. I wondered if he would teach me how to fell a tree.

"Well, thank you George, that was real kind of you," Max said. Dad shrugged and threw the chainsaw into the truck bed. It landed with a thud. He promised Max that he would come back for the wood in a few days. We left shortly after, never venturing any farther into the ranch property. I longingly looked down the road that led to the former Rough House—it was dappled with shade and thimbleberry brambles grew thickly along the edges.

Sitting next to me in the truck, Dad smelled like the forest. I felt proud of him, but also pity. Clearly this was the work he wanted to do, but the number of years he could do this work were waning. He was seventy-four years old. Old age was like that bloody gash he had had—it would slow him down, make everything more dangerous. I wondered what would happen when one day he no longer had a place in the forest.

That night I got an earful about Satan again and another example about how the woods up on the ranch were possessed.

"I was clearing trees out there with my girlfriend," he told me. I was seated on the couch/bed again. Not his high school sweetheart, another girlfriend who was Native American. My dad claimed she could sense when a herd of elk was moving through an area. She and Dad didn't last either: Dad, like my mom, never remarried. "And I was finishing one of the trees on an uphill incline and my girlfriend yelled, 'George! Look out!'" He paused for effect. "Goddamn tree was flying straight *up* the hill, coming right for me! I did a forward somersault, and barely got out of the way in time. Whoever heard of a tree flying *up* a hill?"

Exhausted from listening, and still feeling no connection to my dad, I kissed his forehead goodnight.

"I love you, babes," my dad said.

"I love you too," I recited. But saying "I love you" felt fake.
I didn't even know him.

I wandered out to my tent. I saw Dad turn off his light,
settle into the sleeping bag on the couch to sleep. I wanted to
share stories with my dad, not listen to a monologue. Bill was
in the tent, wearing a headlamp, reading his book.

"Hey," he said.

"Hey," I answered. Bill was so calm, so grounded compared to my dad—and me. My mind was racing. Our idea had
been to stay with my dad for a week, then drive to West Virginia. At the family reunion I was planning on checking out
Bill's genetic lines. But now that I had seen my dad, I was
seriously starting to question my own genes.

"Are we still going to have a kid?" Bill asked, as if he read
my mind.

I sighed. "I wonder if we can even get pregnant," I said.

I had come all this way to my dad's house hoping that we
would have made a connection. I had hoped that I would find
the perfect moment to tell him that Bill and I were going to
become parents, and that even though he hadn't been part of
my life, I wanted him to be a good grandfather. But I hadn't
gotten closer to him; in fact, I felt repulsed. Still, I clung to
the idea that we could connect by going fly-fishing.

The next day I reminded him about the time we went fly-
fishing in Idaho Falls. He didn't seem keen on the concept,
and only halfheartedly rooted around the house looking for
hooks and flies. We went out to the wood-drying shed to look
for his fishing rod. I asked about the furry pelt hanging from
the shed door.

There's a classic photo of Dad tanning an elk hide on the
ranch, the hunting dogs watching him. I figured he was up to

some hide tanning at his cabin. "Is that a beaver?" I asked, pointing to the fur. He looked surprised, and looked at the pelt. "What? Oh, I don't remember. Someone put it there."

Then he resumed rustling around, searching through an odd assortment of books and supplies. Finally, he turned to me and fessed up: "I don't have my fishing license anymore."

He had turned in his Idaho driver's license in exchange for an Arizona one. Out-of-state fishing licenses were expensive, so he hadn't bought a new one. It was then that I remembered the rod and reel from our fishing expedition in Idaho Falls years earlier. Had that been his one and only rod? I hadn't brought it with me. I hadn't even considered that he might need it back.

Instead of going fishing, we resolved to visit the Clearwater River. My dad tossed a green plastic contraption into the back of the truck, then a pair of orange swim trunks, and we loaded into his truck.

The Clearwater is the river of my childhood. It is the marker by which I judge every river I encounter. It is green and cold, and tastes vegetal, like willow water. It is also filled with fish, and as a child I landed my first (and last, as it happens) rainbow trout on its white sandy shores. Out of the white sand grows a species of willow from which we would, as children, harvest branches with pupating caterpillars attached. At home we would put the branches in jars and watch chrysalises form over a series of agonizing days for us. "When will it hatch?" my sister and I would ask my mom over and over again. Eventually, it would, and out would flap a brilliant orange butterfly—a monarch. We would release it from the porch of the Rough House, and the butterfly would have a long journey back to the river.

We drove toward Zan's, a public swimming area along

the Clearwater with a wide sandy beach. As we approached, there were dozens of cars parked along the side of the road and at the impromptu parking lot.

"Too crowded, babes," my dad said and flipped a U-turn.

I looked back at the beach with longing. It wasn't that crowded. Instead we went to the other side of town, to a flat spot along the railroad tracks. Disgruntled, I waded out into the river. It turned out that the green plastic thing my dad had brought along was for panning for gold. The town, Orofino, is named for the flakes of gold in the Clearwater River. But most of it is just fool's gold.

Dad gave Bill a demonstration, and Bill unenthusiastically panned for a while. Nothing. Dad seemed nervous and just watched us; he didn't go in the water at all. He paced around by the road we parked next to. Eventually he came back with a frown-faced woman who told us we were on private property. We packed into the truck and went home, skunked, again. I was starting to see a pattern—every attempt to engage with my dad was leading to a discouraging dead end.

Back at the cabin, Dad and I took a walk. He showed me the almost-ripe huckleberries and we ate a few. We rounded a corner and came across a logging road, which we wandered down. Before long, we encountered the mangled scene of a modern logging operation. There was a pile of dead wood stacked up tall, strips of bark unfurling off the stack. Clods of clay clung to everything. It was like a big monster had come in and devastated this piece of forest.

My dad fell to his knees at this sight, though he must have seen this clear-cut before. "This is a desecration!" he shouted. I looked at the destruction. It was fearsome. Whole trees were stacked on top of each other, creating a twisted, ten-foot wall of gnarled roots and branches. The rest of the area was completely void of vegetation, just reddish brown soil, rippled with bulldozer tracks.

"What happens when you cut like this is the sun bakes the ground," Dad said. He paced in front of the clear-cut like he had the night talking about the cops. He was breathing hard and seemed shaken.

"They'll come in and burn this," he said, pointing at the tree shrapnel. "The ground bakes solid as a rock down two feet." He grabbed his head in his hands. I looked at him, framed in front of the destroyed trees. He took everything so personally. I wondered what had happened to him, what had gone wrong.

"What a waste," he said. Then he showed me how he would go in to salvage some of the logs from the pile before they burned it. So this was where he got the wood to sell by the cord—from scrounging after a logging company's clear-cut.

He wasn't an apex predator, I thought, looking at his stricken face. My dad was a bottom-feeder. He hated this clear-cut yet he made a living from it. He couldn't live in normal society, and so he had to salvage what he could. For my whole life I had imagined him soaring like a hawk, living as one with nature, tall and proud. He was living with nature, but it wasn't proud and romantic. It was messy and sad.

Bill made eggs and potatoes for dinner that night, and I arranged the last of our dried fruit and my homemade cheese on a plate. Hot, in the tiny kitchen, I was wearing a tank top. My dad came in humming to snatch a piece of cheese from the plate. "Oh, that's good," he whistled, and kissed my cheek. I smiled with pride. Then he spotted something on my shoulder, a mole I was born with. He mistook it for a piece of something and picked at it with his thumb and index finger. "It's a mole," I told him, my sympathy for him turning to anger. If he had been around, he would have known my moles, I fumed.

Instead of letting him talk about Satan, I steered Dad toward music, and the guitars he had been building. The big blocks of wood by the door were for making guitars, he explained. While we talked he compulsively cut his fingernails with a pair of clippers down to the quick. Some of them bled.

I remembered another story that Phil, one of the happy hippies at Farm Out, related to me. There had been a winter party at my parents' ranch. My mom had organized it, trying to keep the Idaho winter blues at bay. One by one the hippies arrived, forging through the snow, bringing jugs of wine and dishes of food to share. A few, like Phil and a guitar player, John, brought their instruments. After a feast and a few joints, Phil and John got out their instruments and strummed a few folk songs, noodled a little blue grass while the dishes were being washed. They saw my dad's guitars and asked him to join in. My dad, normally shy, picked up his guitar, a deep golden one, and tuned up. There was a crackling fire, and it had grown dark. He played slowly, quietly, at first—Phil remembered it was a Spanish guitar piece. Soon the entire room was vibrating with the warmth of the guitar, its haunting crescendos and small yelps from my dad guiding the song—being guided by the guitar. "He just blew us away," Phil told me. "We couldn't believe we knew anyone that good."

Now he had no one to listen to his playing except the trees and the squirrels. Hoping to get him out of his crazy mode, I asked him to play for me like he had played for the hippies, like he had played into my tape recorder in Idaho Falls. But he shook his head and held up his hands.

"It's hard to be a woodsman and keep my hands in good condition to play," Dad explained and showed me his calluses from chopping wood. He couldn't play now—he would wait until he got to Arizona. His hands represented perfectly his crippling duality—lover of music must work in the woods in order to survive and make music but can't because the woods are hard on his hands.

He opened up a guitar case and fished out a half-finished guitar. "I am a student of Bouchet," he explained, and showed me how he shaped the guitar's body and attached the neck. The guitar was exquisite, golden, with a carefully inlaid pattern up the neck. It was shockingly beautiful, especially in the squalor of his cabin, as if he had pulled out a diamond necklace from a stinky hobo satchel.

"Do you want this when I'm finished building it?" he asked.

"No," I said, gazing at the beautiful instrument. I couldn't believe someone's hands could make such a thing. I felt bad, ungrateful for rejecting his guitar. "I mean, I don't play, so it will be wasted," I explained.

When I was nineteen I had actually taken guitar classes for a few months. My dad sent me letters with cash in them, encouraging me to take lessons. I found a place just off University Avenue in Seattle and attended a one-on-one class with a bespectacled classical guitar teacher. My maestro would give me assignments from a basic classical guitar book—an adagio perhaps—with the idea that I would practice at home and then could play the piece at the next lesson. I wouldn't study and arrived unprepared, clumsily working my fingers on the strings.

"Your money," the teacher would say. But actually it was my dad's money. I didn't know it at the time, but it was cash extracted from the forest, hard-won, sweat-covered. Unfortunately, both nature and nurture conspired against me. My father's musical and linguistic abilities had not passed on to me and I had no dedication. Feeling bitter—sure that I could have been a guitar player if Dad had actually been around and taught me how to play—I stopped going to lessons and admitted defeat.

"I gave Mother a guitar," he said proudly. "God almighty it was gorgeous. I think it was the only time she was proud of me," he said. He went broody, thinking of his failed mother.

I met Grandmother Jeanne only a few times—my mom made it a point that we would at least know our grandmother. But she was a cold woman who chain-smoked Pall Malls and seemed indifferent to me and my sister. Her house felt like a mausoleum—lifeless and sterile, the exact opposite of Dad. She slept with the radio blaring call-in talk shows. And the only story I remember her telling was the time when she saw a UFO outside of the grocery store. It was purple, with lots of lights. When she was dying from emphysema my sister and I went to her bedside in the hospital. When she saw us her eyes lit up and she scribbled out a note and handed it to me. The note didn't read "I love you" or "I'm at peace," like it's supposed to in the movies. It said, "Oxygen!" and she underlined the word. Dad never reconciled with her, and didn't attend her funeral.

I've been told that I have Grandmother Jeanne's eyes and eyebrows. Deep set, with thick, caterpillaring eyebrows. I wondered if it was odd for him to look at me: his estranged daughter with his estranged mother's eyes.

I awoke the next morning with a feeling of dread. My father and I were just repeating the mistakes of the past. I couldn't see a way out of the cycle. I had come here to tell him about my plans to have children. To resolve the issues I had with him before moving on to become a mother. But he wasn't willing—or able. So perhaps it was with a touch of frustration that I picked a fight with my dad that morning, making it the first brawl in the history of our relationship at ages seventy-four and thirty-seven.

Somehow we got onto the topic of my mom.

"I would come home from a ten- to twelve-hour day," he said, "and I'd come home to her hatred. No dinner. No praise. Just criticism," Dad said, detailing why my mom didn't work out as a good wife for him. I sat in the only chair in the house, by the window; Bill was outside, still asleep.

It was as if their split had happened just days before, his anger was so raw. It set me on edge, flutters of fear rippled down my stomach.

"So, you weren't really interested in being a dad?" I asked. It was only after the words came out of my mouth that I felt a choking, blinding anger welling up in me—stored so long, now unleashed.

Suddenly Dad felt the need to sweep his particleboard floor. "Then she would call Rick, and say she wanted to learn how to cut down trees," he said, ignoring my question. "She was so competitive." He kept sweeping. "All she had to do was be a wife, raise you guys, make food, sew, whatever. She could do whatever she wanted, but she had to be competitive."

From my mom's account of life on the ranch, she hadn't exactly been living a life of leisure. She chopped wood, kept the woodstove burning, milked the cow, fed the ducks and chickens, breast-fed us, and cleaned the house. That she wanted to help my dad log the land—no doubt for some much needed cash—seemed like a rather generous offer. But I was starting to notice that my dad, wild man that he projected himself as—was just a traditionalist when it came to gender roles. He wanted my mom barefoot, pregnant, and subservient.

"Then she brought that cretin into our bed," he snarled. The day of the big fight with the lemonade. My hazy memory of the fight was later explained to me—first by Dad when I was in my twenties. According to Dad, on a fall day in 1975 he had returned to the Rough House after a long absence. He did this often, just disappearing for weeks on end. Duward the carpenter was there and Dad flew into a rage. He and the woodworker had a face-off: Dad pulled a gun, Duward had just a two-by-four. The two men stood, almost touching chests. Finally Dad muttered, "It's not worth it," and lowered his gun. Duward turned and ran.

Then Dad came into the kitchen and Riana and I warded him away from Mom.

Mom met Duward when she started selling fresh cow milk to the neighbors—she had excess milk and wanted the money to buy building supplies so they could finish the house. Duward was one of her milk customers, and eventually became her boyfriend.

"You guys were home, and she brought that cretin into our bed," he shrieked. "I was going to burn the house down," he said. "Burn everything."

Including us. I felt another wave of fear. The neighbor started firing his guns. Loud ricocheting bullet sounds added to our discussion.

My fear morphed into a red-hot rage. "Why are you blaming me for something between my mom and you?" I yelled. I wondered if Bill, sleeping in the tent, would hear our argument.

My dad started crying. A deep shuddering cry. He leaned

against his broom. "We just need to forgive each other," he said.

My hackles rose. Wait a minute, this man had abandoned me, and I should be asking for forgiveness?

"I don't think you have anything to forgive me for," I yelled and stood up. "I haven't done anything wrong." Then I thought about Bill and our future children and blurted out, "I know that if I had a kid, I wouldn't fucking abandon it like you did to us. And neither would Bill!" Even as I said it, I wasn't sure I believed it.

I went into the kitchen and started throwing stuff around, grabbed our kitchen supplies, and threw them into the camping box. There were two identical cast iron pans on the stove. One was coated with egg from last night's dinner. I grabbed the clean one.

I walked outside with our stuff, fuming. Bill was just emerging from the tent, hair tousled. I tossed the camping box of food into the backseat of the car. "We're leaving!" I yelled to Bill. My dad stood on the porch, watching. I stuffed my sleeping bag and grabbed the Therm-a-Rests from under Bill and carried them to the car.

Bill slowly started to break down the tent, but he wasn't moving fast enough for me. I bumped him out of the way. "Go start the car," I huffed. I pulled the tent down and, not bothering to fold it, threw the whole thing into the backseat.

The Benz roared to life with a puff of smoke, and we were backing up out of George Carpenter's driveway.

After a few miles of driving, Bill cleared his throat. "Things didn't go well?"

We were at a four-way stop, about to turn onto the main road. Back on the road, mission oh so unsuccessful.

"My dad's a fucking asshole," I spit. "He's a nut job. What the hell is wrong with him?"

"He did seem really out there," Bill said, trying to calm me down. He eased the car forward, and we heard a terrible clunking noise.

The car stalled in the middle of the intersection.

"Oh, shit," Bill muttered.

"What? What?" I said. Were we breaking down? I leaped out of the car and we pushed it onto the side of the road. Bill started the engine but the car couldn't go forward. He crawled under the car to take a look and instructed me to shift the gears.

"It's the rear tail shaft," he said grimly, scooting out.

We sat in the car. He knew because he had just worked on a customer's vehicle that needed a new tail shaft in the transmission and he recognized the sound. We could tow it into town, but the part is rare—a 1976 Mercedes Benz rear tail shaft?

"The funny thing is," Bill said, "I have two at our house." He had brought a spare alternator, headlights, and an extra battery, but didn't think we'd need a rear tail shaft.

Then I saw a truck pull up behind us. My heart sank— Dad.

He jumped out of his truck and went into hero mode. Without a word, he grabbed a big chain out of the back of his truck, hitched it to our car, then pulled his truck around and connected it.

"I know a guy in town," he said. I knew that Dad would have done this for anyone with car trouble, it wasn't just because I was his daughter. It's part of Idaho life: If you see someone who needs help, you help. On the day I was born, Mom was driving herself to the hospital when the rear axle fell off the Jeep. A kindly Idaho stranger stopped to save the day.

Dad towed us fourteen miles to Village Auto, a little shop by the Clearwater River. He went in to talk to Dan, the owner of the shop. Dan agreed Bill could use his garage to fix the car for a small sum. My dad unchained the truck, then tipped his hat, Clint Eastwood style, and drove away.

We were stuck in Orofino.

Retracing my parents' footsteps,
Novella and Bill in Mexico, 1998.

Seven

Bill and I drank some jasmine tea and dipped our feet in the Clearwater River. We were at a campground just outside of Orofino called the Pink House Hole, which, to me, sounded vaguely vaginal. The hole had been a favorite fishing spot for locals before they tore down the eponymous pink house and turned it into an official recreation site. Fourteen bucks a night. I wasn't going to go back to my dad's house—and I doubt I would be invited back. Bill figured it would be two days before our part arrived.

"Want to go for a walk?" Bill asked.

"Sure," I said.

We found ourselves along some railroad tracks. Picking blackberries. "We could've slept here," Bill said, pointing to a nest of brambles. Bill has always wanted to be a hobo. His aesthetic—ripped clothes, dirty T-shirts—is pure bum.

His scruffiness was one of the first things I liked about him when he got on an elevator with me in Seattle in 1998. I was twenty-five, working on the UW campus for Classroom Support Services. After seven on and off years of college, I had finally graduated and had lingered around campus working as an AV tech, paid small sums of money to push PLAY on VCRs for classes. In the elevator, Bill, a new employee, recently arrived from Florida, was wearing a too-small blue sweatshirt and a red mohair hat that slumped over his lush dark hair. I sported a peeling turquoise pleather jacket and horn-rimmed glasses. He seemed nervous, which I liked. Later he sent me an e-mail that said I was intriguing and he asked me out. Our first date involved meeting in a back alley to eat sardines balanced on saltine crackers we had filched from the student cafeteria. We moved in together after the second date.

Channeling my parents, our first winter together Bill and I traveled to Mexico. After some time in Oaxaca, on my insistence, we headed to San Miguel de Allende. Bill and I arrived by a Semi-Directo bus. *So this is where my parents met?* I thought, filled with emotion when the bus pulled into the ancient town, the giant cathedral curlicuing up to the blue Mexican sky. *This is where it all started.*

Overcome with the weight of the past and its implications, I missed the last step off the bus and tumbled—a twenty-five-year-old gringa, giant yellow backpack strapped on like a beetle's carapace, spinning through the air, trying to regain my footing. I landed with a thud on the cobblestones. The bus driver laughed, he couldn't help himself. Bill tried not to do the same, and carried me to the youth hostel. I was distraught, and sat with my foot up in the hostel's common room, immobilized. Bill went out to explore, and when he came back he said there were lots of Americans living there. It was no longer the undiscovered oasis of my parents' youth.

We left a few days later. I limped onto the bus and we headed to the coast where I could heal up. Propped up at the beach, I felt like a failure. Not just because I hadn't gotten to explore the town where my parents first met but because my future seemed so dingy and uninspiring compared to my parents' younger years.

It was in that winter, 1998, just after our failed San Miguel de Allende trip, that Bill met my dad for the first time.

We were in Bill's VW, driving through the Southwest. I had unfolded a map of Arizona, a cup of coffee between my legs; Bill was smoking a hand-rolled Drum cigarette. "Hey, we're near Wickenburg!" I said.

"So?" Bill answered. The cactus-filled landscape seemed to go on forever.

"I think my dad's there," I said, remembering that he sent me a postcard mentioning that he was staying at the Purple Hills Apartments. I was learning to be a writer then, and his life seemed a proper one for an artist. I heavily romanticized his decision to never join mainstream America. I had been bragging to Bill about my cool dad, playing down the fact that we were estranged. I hadn't seen him for more than an hour since 1984. "Let's go see him!" Bill said. I smiled. Bill was writing poetry then, he was thin as a rail.

We pulled into the dusty parking lot of the Purple Hills Apartments. I stared at the buildings. One of the "apartments" was a teepee staked in the backyard. I figured the teepee had to be my dad's. I climbed out of the bus and stood near the entrance, trying to determine how to knock on the door of a teepee.

Before I could make an attempt, he came out of apartment number 3 in his socks, perplexed about the wheezing VW bus in his parking lot.

He hadn't changed that much since the last time I had seen him, almost a decade before. He still had dark hair and a mustache. He was thin and bandy, his face angular and haggard. He wore a down vest—it was chilly, even in Arizona, during the winter.

"Dad, it's Novella," I called, wondering if he would recognize me. I'd sent him photos, of course, but I wasn't sure he would make the connection. He let out a whistle and I walked over to give him a hug.

In my dad's apartment we drank some screw-top Gallo wine that my dad pulled out of the mini-fridge. After catching up on things, we got on the topic of the existence of aliens. Dad had gotten into listening to a radio show hosted by Art Bell, who often talked about paranormal activities and pseudoscience. When Dad went to the bathroom, I snuck a peek into his bedroom. He had lined the windows with aluminum foil and had a spartan bed covered with an old sleeping bag. There was a shortwave radio for entertainment, but other than that, it seemed a monkish existence.

Bill and I were just getting together, and I had taken it as a good sign that he had wanted to meet my dad. It wasn't the usual dad-meets-beau scenario, all uncomfortable in the living room with the father finally asking, "What are your intentions with my daughter, son?" No, it was aliens and bad wine. Bill and I stayed only a few hours—we had more adventures ahead of us that we were eager to get to.

As we pulled away, waving, I asked Bill: "What did you think of him?" I was actually wondering what I thought of him myself. At the time I harbored no hard feelings about his absence from my life—I was twenty-five, resilient, haphazard, self-absorbed.

"He's weird but cool," Bill said in his raspy voice. I nodded in agreement. Later, I would make a photo album of Bill and my trip, and my dad makes an appearance in it. Under a shot of him I scrawled, "This is George Elliott Carpenter. He uses an old sock for an oven mitt and a stove rack for an antennae for his radio."

Back then, I saw Dad as an example of living simply, in voluntary poverty. He was still part of the sixties counterculture that I had grown up admiring. The hippie movement, celebrated in PBS specials and in my mom's stories, seemed heroic to me. My generation—Gen X? Slackers? The MTV generation?—didn't even have a name that stuck. We listened to indie rock and went to rallies to ban plastic water bottles. But these actions piddled out, never blossomed into a full-fledged student uprising like they had in the sixties. Maybe there just weren't enough of us. Born in the shadow of that era, I always felt like my formative years were a collection of little side projects that didn't add up to a fully realized movement that could match up to my mom's glory days in Berkeley, or Mom and Dad's foreign adventures.

While Bill and I walked along the tracks in Orofino, stuck now for who knows how long, I thought about how we had been inspired by how Dad was living back then. His shabby room at the Purple Hills struck me as artistic, heroic to me as a young person. The way he was balancing his life as a mountain man in Idaho with his time in Arizona struck me as particularly genius. Since then, he hadn't changed much—but I had.

My phone rang. A 208 area code, an Idaho number.

"Hello?" I answered, worried it might be my dad.

"Hey, it's Lowell. Are you on the railroad tracks?" Lowell, from Farm Out, said in his deep rumbly voice. Someone—my mom?—had gotten word to him that we were in town and had given him my phone number.

"Yeah," I said.

"I'm in the truck right behind you."

I laughed and looked over and saw a grizzled old guy sitting behind the wheel of a big white pickup truck. I hadn't seen Lowell in years.

"We're broken down," I told him when we got to his truck. Lowell looked like how I remembered him from the Farm Out days, healthy and fit. His eyes, which are almost Asian in shape, still twinkled mischievously, he just had some more wrinkles around the edges. The beard was gone, as were the flowing long blond locks. He was wearing a baseball cap. I remembered how, at Farm Out, he and Tom used to take off their shirts and wrestle. They also bopped bellies. Running toward each other, they would jump into the air, belly flesh bumping into belly flesh, followed by roars of laughter. My sister and I, sheltered on the ranch as we were, watched them in awe. I had never seen men act like that, playing, having fun, like children.

"Wanna come up and see my place?" he asked.

We said sure and before long we were driving along the windy road up to Farm Out. As we drove, Lowell pointed out attractions along the mullein-lined road. There was the massive Dworshak Dam and a bar called The Woodlot. Lowell, unlike many of the hippies, had really got to know the Orofino locals. He would ask them for planting advice, livestock tips.

He was the only Farm Out hippie left—maybe because he had made those connections.

It took twenty minutes of concentrated driving—dodging potholes, taking sharp hairpin turns—before we got up to the gravel road of the Farm Out property. "I must've done this drive ten thousand times," Lowell said.

"You still having those solstice parties?" I asked. Thinking of the fires and the naked people, the belly-bopping.

"Oh, no," he grumbled. "They got too big. The whole damn town would show up, and my new wife put an end to that."

"That was the first house we all lived in," he said, pointing to a two-story clapboard house. When the commune first started, Lowell, Marcia, Phil, and Tom all lived together in the main house. It was painted red and looked homey. Acres of grass spilled out behind it. There were a few outbuildings and homemade-looking structures that were built when the happy hippies realized they needed more space, especially as the commune grew and stragglers showed up.

"I ended up selling it after our divorce," he said. Lowell and Marcia, his first wife, had split around the same time as my mom and my dad.

"Now it's some survivalist types living there. They came for Y2K, then when nothing happened, they just stayed." Some dogs came by and chased the tires of the truck at a flat stretch along the road.

"Where did you guys keep the goats?" I asked. The place didn't look exactly as I had remembered it.

"Over there in that field," Lowell pointed to a shrubby golden field.

On the left, underneath a stand of ponderosa pine, was a

rustic-looking shack. It was more in keeping with what I thought my dad's place would be like, how Glahn's cabin would look.

"What's that?" Bill asked.

"That's Phil's cabin," Lowell said and smiled. "We were all living in that house, and you know, after a while we all realized we needed some privacy so we could have sex or do whatever, so Phil built that cabin." Phil's a college professor now—English, at the University of Idaho. He comes to Orofino regularly, though, to hang out with Lowell.

Phil, like Tom, Marcia, and the other happy hippies, had realized in their own ways that they couldn't last on this remote piece of land. Winters were especially brutal up there. Sometimes they had to snowshoe into town for supplies, and no one had four-by-four trucks back in that time. The only airline out of town, Cascade Airlines, was in Lewiston but had been dubbed Crashcades. There was no way out for the duration of the winter, which was long in Idaho. For some reason Lowell stayed. He worked in the woods, lumberjacking, then started a construction business. To supplement his income, he drove a school bus. During the summer he helped lead whitewater rafting trips on the Clearwater and other nearby tributaries. He wasn't rich, but he had found a way to live off the land and pay the bills.

We continued down the gravel road until Lowell said, "And that is my house."

He parked the truck outside of a beautiful, three-story log cabin. We went inside. It had huge blond beams and picture windows with views of the mountains. We went up to the top floor, into a big open kitchen. It was like being in a giant tree house. Over the years Lowell had devoted himself to building this enormous homestead. Spread out below was the rest of his farm—the horse stalls and other outbuildings, several pigs and chickens, hutches for his daughter's pet rabbits, and a giant vegetable garden. Surveying it all, I suddenly felt a wave of sadness: this was what the Rough House was supposed to have been.

"This is Maya and Jasmen," Lowell said when two curly-haired teenagers came upstairs. They went to Orofino High. The Maniacs, their high school mascot, they explained when I brought it up, had nothing to do with the insane asylum next door. I nodded; maybe I had gotten that story wrong.

Lowell had always been adamant about not wanting to have children during his Farm Out days. He even had a vasectomy when he was with Marcia. But then, in his fifties, he met a younger woman who wanted children. He reversed the vasectomy and against the odds, sired two daughters. Maya had his twinkly eyes.

"So what brings you to Orofino?" Lowell asked.

I told him about my disastrous visit with my dad.

"I see your dad around town sometimes," Lowell said. "He's always been cordial. But then again, I don't know if he recognizes me. He is a real character," Lowell said.

"Yeah," I said.

"Right. He could have found work, and led a normal life—but he never did."

"Never compromised," I sighed. "For what that's worth."

"I think for him," Lowell said, "that's worth a lot."

After lunch we took a walk around the farm. We saw the bricks where the kiln had been, the area where the fire pit had burned for the solstice parties. It all seemed vaguely familiar.

"Where are the bees?" I asked. I remembered Lowell's hives dotting the Farm Out property, and that he often smelled like honey and wax after a day of tending to his hives.

His father had been a commercial beekeeper in upstate New York, and he carried the skill with him to Idaho.

"Got foulbrood," he said and shook his wooly head. American foulbrood is a contagious bacterial infection that germinates in the bee larvae, eventually dooming the hive. There is no cure. "Had to burn all my hives." He paused, laughing at the memory, "So of course I had a party, a bonfire. You can't believe the colors those hives let off. Must've been the different kinds of pollen, but it was like Fourth of July."

He looked sad, but it wasn't because of the bees: He and his second wife were getting a divorce. Things had just not worked out. He was fighting for custody of his daughters.

"They seem sweet," I said. They looked so different from the Oakland teens with their tight skirts and giant dangling earrings. And from me and my sister as teenagers in the 1980s, when we were into clothes and had big hair.

I remembered that at that age I was especially embarrassed about our house, which looked nothing like the mansion of my dreams. It was more of a hippie den. Mom's boyfriend Tom sent artifacts from his soil science research trips to Mali and Indonesia: batik fabrics, carved wooden statues, and masks of African faces. Mom hung the masks from the wall and covered the stairwells with the fabric. She made us listen to world music too, when all we wanted to hear was Duran Duran.

Wearing her Jesse Jackson for President T-shirt, digging around in her garden, Mom regarded our mall-rat behavior with concern. She didn't know it, but I had taken up drinking by the time I was fourteen. Peach-flavored California Coolers were my poison, provided by friends' older brothers. Remembering my big hair and California Cooler days in Shelton, I wondered what teenagers in rural areas were into these days.

"They are good kids," Lowell nodded. "And if I have to pay for them, I want to actually see them."

I felt a pang of envy. My dad hadn't wanted to do either—pay for us, or see us. Child support was a big battle between my mom and dad. He only started making regular child support payments while I was in high school—from 1986 to 1991. The height of my materialist years. I never thought about where the money came from that my dad sent, I just deposited the folded bills into my bank account and looked forward to going shopping. But now I knew: cord-wood money, scrapped and gleaned, sweat-soaked bills.

Every once in a while my mom would mutter something about how my sister and I were too materialistic, but we would roll our eyes. My sister and I had her outnumbered. My mom's hippie era of free love and student protests had fallen away, replaced by the greed-is-good eighties. She held out, though, kind of like Lowell had, in her own way. She put up solar water-heating panels on the house, grew a vegetable garden on the side of the house. It was all about small gestures of rebellion.

"Hey, Lowell," I said after the tour was over. "Is this going to be Sunset Acres?" My mom and her hippie friends had had a retirement scheme: as they grew older, they would buy land together and hire a nurse to take care of everyone until they kicked the bucket. This plan was hatched while they were still too young and healthy to really know what it would be like later on in their lives—the cancers and the pain, the operations and the general decay of their once healthy bodies. It seemed like a joke back then, growing old.

Driving back to town, Lowell took a different route. He paused at one particularly scenic point. Somehow there was a wheat field high up in the Orofino hills. "It's the last of the

Palouse," he said, pointing west. The Palouse is the huge wheat growing area that covers eastern Washington and creeps into Idaho. It doesn't get far into Idaho though, because it becomes too mountainous, too wild for cultivating wheat.

I looked at Lowell and remembered something his friend Phil had told me about what it had been like to be young and living in the woods at Farm Out. They felt invincible, he said, free and big, and they made good money and got roaring drunk and smoked cigs and arm wrestled and people respected them because they worked in the woods. Now Lowell was driving the school bus and slowing down.

"The last of the Palouse," Lowell said and sighed, and drove us back to our campground.

Bill's and my first night at Pink House Hole Campground was pleasant. We discovered, from the drunken campground host, that the site may have been where Lewis and Clark had spent a long cold winter. The Nez Percé Indians helped the poor guys build five canoes and redirected them westward. After Lewis and Clark came the miners, then the homesteaders, and then the hippies. In fact, my parents had camped right along these shores forty years ago, when they were looking to buy property in Orofino.

The closer I looked at my parents' past, the better I was able to see the parallels in my own life. It was starting to freak me out.

In 2001, Bill and I were living in Seattle. We both had good jobs—I worked for a travel-book publishing company, he had become an auto mechanic and worked on taxicabs. Then 9/11 hit; I lost my job a few days after the Twin Towers fell. A week later, Bill came home with all his tools: No one was taking cabs anymore, and they laid him off. We had money saved, and I had a severance, so we decided to go to Europe. Remembering my parents and their good times in Formentera, we bought plane tickets to Spain.

Thinking we could make more of a connection to Spanish culture, we signed up as WOOFers—Willing Workers on Organic Farms. The deal was we would work on a farm for four hours a day, and the farm would give us a place to stay and feed us. I hoped I could learn something about farming— we had been dabbling with beekeeping and had chickens and a vegetable garden in our Seattle backyard—and I wanted to learn more. Instead of learning how to farm, though, we ended up washing dishes at a "farmer's" restaurant. At another "farm" we were employed by British expats to clean up a house that had been infested with rats while the owner was on vacation. Poison had been put out; our job was to clean up the resulting carnage. We found dead rats in drawers, kitchen cabinets, in the knitting basket. We burned everything. Not really farming, I thought, throwing another rat corpse in the burn barrel.

We ended up buying bicycles and biked along the Spanish coast. Some areas were beautiful: We would pull over next to the perfectly blue Mediterranean and go skinny dipping. We bought homebrewed wine from gnarled old guys and put the bottles in our bikes' water bottle holders. We had fun but I kept comparing Spain in the early aughts to the Spain of 1970, of my parents' experience. Instead of rustic, cheap living, we kept running up against touristy paella restaurants and Flamenco dancer postcards. The island of Formentera, once pristine, had become a high-end tourist destination.

After Spain, our next plan involved moving to the Bay

Area. We were sick of the rain, and all our friends were set-
tling down, buying houses, and having kids. We still wanted
to have some adventures. Oakland seemed like the perfect
place to do that. It was relatively cheap and had a funky sensi-
bility that made me feel at home. We packed our van full of
our possessions—mostly vinyl records and our cat, Sparkles—
and drove south. In Oakland we eventually rented a falling-
down duplex off of Martin Luther King Jr. Way. Only later
I realized that my mom had, in her Berkeley days, lived on
MLK back when it was called Grove Street, and Dad had lived
in West Oakland, by the port, with some other musicians—
making my apartment roughly halfway between their former
houses. A few years later, I would attend UC Berkeley: just like
my parents had.

Sometimes when I look back on past events like these, I
recognize certain characteristics that seem to resurface from
my parents' past to my own. We share wanderlust, a DIY
spirit, and a tendency for romanticizing poverty. Characters
reappear too. Some of my close friends remind me of the people I met as a kid at Farm Out. The longer I'm alive, the pres-
ent starts to look like an anagram of the past. It's a different
pattern using the same elements. There's a Mark Twain quote
that captures the same idea: "The past doesn't repeat, but it
does rhyme."

Bill and I snuggled up in the tent, a vicious wind blowing
in up the river. What a day. Back then, when my parents had
camped along this very river, poised to buy the ranch, my
mom had been pregnant with Riana. Would I get pregnant
here in Orofino, like my mom got pregnant with me, setting
in motion the next generation? I wondered if the salmon ever
felt like this when they returned from the ocean, snuffling
around the river rocks, smelling around for home, looking for

a place to lay their eggs. Was I capable of reproducing? I was beginning to wonder.

Bill and I spent the next day at the Orofino library, checking our e-mail and reading books. The librarians were excruciatingly kind to us. As I was catching up with a few days' worth of e-mail, I realized that the carrel—there was only one—I was sitting in was exactly where my dad sat and wrote his e-mail missives to me. There was a world political map poster tacked to the wall of the carrel, and I wondered if Dad daydreamed looking at it, remembering Spain and Mexico and France. As I imagined him sitting there, I found that my anger toward him had cooled. But it was replaced with confusion. Why was he so broken? What had happened to him?

In my inbox was a forwarded message from my sister from Dad, probably written that morning at this same computer terminal while Bill and I slept in the Hole. It said that he was worried about me; he wrote that "she tore into me like a cur dog" and that I seemed to be in an emotional nosedive.

As I read the e-mail, my hackles rose again—I didn't attack him!

Or did I?

The truth was, I had been caught by surprise by my dad and his circumstances. I had always assumed that my father had been absent from my life because he had chosen the higher ground; that he was living the righteous life of a mountain man hermit. It was true that his main source of income came from the forest—but from scavenging trees left over from big logging operations. He didn't live a heroic life full of communing with nature. His life was brutal; he was just scraping by, barely surviving. This glimpse of him in his cabin made me realize that he had been hiding something from me for all these years, and it raised a new possibility. I wrote back to my sister, "My latest fear is that Dad is, and has always been, mentally ill." I'll admit it: I wasn't just concerned for Dad. I was concerned for myself, and for my future children.

In the morning, the tail shaft arrived at Village Auto. It took Bill two hours to put in the replacement part. When we tried to pay Dan, he said, "It's been taken care of." My dad.

Then we were back on the road, headed to Bill's family reunion in West Virginia. Rosie belched along, miraculous as ever. As Orofino disappeared into the rearview mirror I felt a rush of relief, glad to be done with my father—if our pattern held—for at least another few years.

My parents at the infamous A-frame in Crescent, Oregon.
Mom five months pregnant, 1971.

Eight

We were on the road, headed East from Orofino, to visit friends and go to Bill's family reunion. As we drove, my ovary erupted, releasing an egg, increasing my mucous levels, spiking my internal body temperature. After a year of trying, I had started observing and charting such data. I alerted Bill. We were somewhere in eastern Montana. We turned off the main road, sped across a dirt track, past newly cut alfalfa fields, past a sign that read WATCH OUT FOR BUGGIES. The hills were sprinkled with trees and pink-striped outcroppings.

After seeing my dad, I wasn't so sure I should be reproducing. He seemed to have some mental issues that could be inheritable. As Bill and I drove, ominous warning signs—literal signs—started to crop up. First, an official, brown governmental-looking road sign that read CHIEF DULL KNIFE COLLEGE. That had to be a joke. Then we passed another sign:

CRAZY HEAD LAKE, with an arrow. My dad was certainly crazy, I thought. Why am I rolling the dice?

Before long we found a private, slow-moving river. It was called, oddly, The Tongue. After a picnic bankside, we settled into the soft sand at the water's edge. Compared to the Clearwater, this river just didn't seem right. It was murky and slow moving. We stripped off our clothes and tried to make a baby. A frog hopped by us. As we were wrapping up, a storm started brewing. Rain drops pelted our naked bodies. The sky got dark and mosquitoes closed in on us. We threw on our clothes and made a dash for the car.

Then the storm really unleashed. Lightning struck the fields right near our car, and we heard the thunder follow immediately. Huge raindrops hit our windshield. The sky turned a strange blue color.

"Do you think we made the gods angry?" I asked Bill as he started the car and pulled away from the river.

He laughed his little cough-laugh. Up ahead on the dirt road, we saw a black horse pulling a black carriage. It looked demonic. A black tarp whipped fiercely over the roof of the buggy. Another bolt of lightning struck a nearby field, lighting up the dark sky.

"Should I honk?" Bill asked, always the smart ass, while we passed the horse-drawn buggy. The horse was a deep chestnut color and wore blinders. Its mane was damp with rain.

"It's kind of evil looking," I said, and turned to see what was inside the tarp-enshrouded buggy. Seated behind the horse was a deathly thin, pale-faced woman clutching the reins with skeletal hands. She looked like the female version of the grim reaper. Her eyes met mine and she scowled. I gasped and looked back at the road, filled with dread: we were going to have a demon baby.

. . .

Bill and I arrived back to Oakland in September, dirty and exhausted. We had been on the road for over three weeks. I opened the front door and schlepped the valuables upstairs to our apartment. It was early in the morning; we had driven all night so we could sleep in our own bed.

When I scanned our long-forgotten apartment, I saw a pile of sticky bee frames in one corner of the living room; in another, Bill's car parts spilled over on a precariously built table. The front deck was aquiver with rabbits, the back porch was loaded with goat poo. Our house was squalid and insane seeming.

Instead of dealing with it, I collapsed into our rumpled bed and fell into a deep sleep. The next morning, I purged the house. Why was I clinging to these bucket lids and such a huge collection of stained towels? When I opened up the freezer, I encountered some rabbit hides that I had been collecting for years. I had always meant to learn how to tan those hides—like my dad had done back on the ranch. Bill and I joked about them, called them skinsicles, but now they seemed creepy, Jeffrey Dahmer–like.

While I hung laundry out to dry on the line outside, I caught a glimpse of our backyard outhouse. We had it built for ecological reasons—a couple years ago I had read a book called *The Toilet Papers* that argued that it was insane to void our wastes into perfectly clean water. With that in mind, we tacked up a simple wooden structure, threw a thirty-five-gallon container underneath a crudely attached toilet seat, and voilà: an outhouse. Unfortunately, it had been a failed experiment, as both Bill and I were too lazy to go outside to use the toilet when we had a perfectly functional one in the house.

The outhouse was filled with cobwebs, not humanure. Still, it wasn't lost on me—I had an outhouse. Just like my dad.

After purging, I read my mail. There was a letter from John Garrick waiting in our mail pile. It was written on yellow lined paper, in neat handwriting. About my dad, he wrote:

> *He was like a butterfly, here today, gone tomorrow type of guy. He was a dreamer, of doing great things, and not afraid to try! Some friends I forget over the years, sometimes I even forget their names. Then there are those friends you carry the friendship in the heart, there you never forget them and want the best for them. I read once—a friend is one who overlooks your broken fence and admires the flowers in your garden. I guess that about describes George and my friendship. He overlooked my faults and I overlooked his. We understood each other and so it is!!*

As I reread the letter, touched that John had written me, I wished that I could have similar Hallmark card–like feelings about my dad. But after our reunion, I was ready to forget about him completely—to overlook both the broken fence and whatever stupid flowers he had growing. What kind of relationship had I hoped to build with him after so many years of neglect, I wasn't sure. Too many years had passed, too many broken promises and missed connections had transpired, I realized, to mend our relationship in just one visit. I had been nurturing an unrealistic and romantic vision of what our reunion would be like, all fly-fishing and catching up on the years that had long passed. Of course it had been a failure. I was ready to give up and stop trying to make a connection that had withered when I was just a little girl.

I blamed my dad, mostly. For his messy, haphazard life. In fact, in purging the house, I felt like I was purging Dad's characteristics out of me.

I sat back and looked out at our squat lot garden from the living room window. The tomato plants had gone feral in our absence and had toppled the rickety tomato cages I had rigged up to support them. The squash plants were rambling across the open areas. A thicket of wild radish had infested the potato patch and was in full, pink bloom.

So far the owner of the property had not stopped us from squat gardening, but I knew one day this would happen and they would build condos. And when that happened, would I then fall to my knees and yell, "This is a desecration!" as my dad had at the sight of that clear-cut? My dad—he logged wood on land that wasn't his, and I raised vegetables and animals on land that wasn't mine either. I cruised for street tree branches, he collected guitar wood. We weren't so different.

Feeling uneasy, I called Mom. She wanted details about Orofino, and my dad. I told her about his cluttered cabin, the paranoid stories.

"It's really sad," she said. "He was so talented."

I asked if he ever seemed crazy.

"He was always moody," she said. "He would have these ups and downs."

"What would he do?" I asked. "When he was down, what would he do?"

"Just sulk and play his guitar," she said. "But he never seemed really crazy. Course my psychologist friend diagnosed him as manic-depressive, but I'm not sure.

"I think I went a little crazy just being with him," she confessed. "I tried to burn the house down once. Well, just theatrics, I got dramatic, I didn't really start a big fire . . ." I remembered my dad telling me at his cabin that he had wanted to burn down the house after he found my mom with the cretin at the Rough House. And my twelve-year-old pyrotechnics. We were a family of pyromaniacs.

She went on: "But I was so frustrated that he wouldn't help finish the house."

They had lived in a trailer for years while they built the Rough House next door, one shingle at a time. Once the house was semi-habitable, they moved in, but it was never quite finished. My mom imagined that life in the big house would be like domestic bliss. Maybe that's why my dad, undomesticated guy that he is, balked at finishing.

After a pause she said, "You know, your dad scared me." Then she told me that when they were living in the A-frame in Crescent, newly together after their courtship in Mexico, he had tried to kill her cat.

He had come home from hunting with his prize: a few ducks. He hung them outside to ripen before plucking them. Somehow, my mom's cat had snatched one of the ducks and dragged it under the house. Dad became so furious, he got his gun out and shot the cat.

"He hit the flap under her arm," she explained, "so he didn't kill her—if he had, I would've left him. But I was so upset. I remember going to the back of the house and crying and crying. I was going to leave. But he convinced me not to."

"It's weird to think," I said after a while, not knowing what to say to my mom on the phone. "That if Dad was a better shot, I wouldn't even exist."

The violence against animals was just a precursor, she told me. "He would just suddenly punch me for no reason," she said. "I had to watch what I said around him. Then one time I woke up in the middle of the night and he had a knife to my throat." And then there was the time he chased her with a shotgun. . . .

As these new, dark stories unfurled, I felt a sinking, horrible sensation. My father was a monster. Why hadn't she told me about this before, why hadn't I noticed—or remembered these things when I was a little girl? Their fight with the lemonade, and Riana and me jumping on his legs. It's one of my earliest memories, and now that I thought about it, a violent one. My early childhood seemed dangerous, suddenly, marked by violence and threats that came from Dad.

Of course Mom was looking for a way out. "I used to always be so worried he might get killed out there doing those thinning jobs," she said. "But toward the end there, I started to hope a tree *would* fall on him."

"Did he ever hit us?" I asked.

"No, not that I knew of," she said. My mouth felt dry and my stomach churned.

That fight at Dad's cabin. Maybe it was a good thing he wasn't an apex predator anymore. But what had made him so violent?

"So, when you saw him, did he say bad things about me?" Mom asked.

"Yes, Mom," I told her, "terrible things." But I wouldn't go into detail. Four years after punishment summer in 1988, when Dad and his girlfriend had broken up and he lost the Rough House, Mom had actually let Dad stay on the property until she could sell it. Because Dad had started paying child support by then, he and Mom had an uneasy truce.

But then, when I was sixteen and Riana was about to graduate from high school, Mom got wind that he was logging on the property. And not just any logs—big ones—the old-growth grove right next to the house. These trees had been a selling point for my young parents. They were the trees I had sat under for hours as a little girl. I remember her angry voice on the phone, talking to lawyers about the illegal logging. She sent him an outraged letter. He sent the letter back to her, scrawling in the margins, spilling out his anger and hate. "Son of a bitch!" she yelled, tossing the letter onto the kitchen table. I snuck a look.

In it, he outlined that he hadn't abused a single square inch of the ranch property. That he has lived without power, water, or a phone; and drove a beat-up truck so we could receive our child support money. He said he did this gladly because we are a product of a deep love, a love that my mom never felt. Then he called my mom a vindictive bitch. The letter became like an anti-talisman; my mom would reread it from time to time, replenishing her anger and hate, any time she started to feel sorry for Dad.

This letter, dated December 7, 1988, would mark the beginning of a disastrous year for Mom. One that she never quite recovered from. She and Tom, after a long-distance but long-term relationship, split up. Things had reached a breaking point. They had talked about moving in together, but my mom was adamant that she wouldn't remarry. They broke up instead. My mom never dated anyone again. "Men—they are just too much trouble," she said. Then her school, Hood Canal School, where she had taught for years, burned to the ground. Arson, though no one was charged. Even the outside political world seemed to be telling my political and environmentally minded Mom "fuck you": George H. W. Bush was elected president; the Exxon Valdez crashed into some rocks in Alaska and caused the biggest oil spill in history. The natural world, the pristine Prince William Sound in Alaska, despoiled by a drunken man.

"What are you trying to find?" Mom finally asked. "Why are you trying to find your dad?"

"I guess I wanted to find the truth, why he hasn't been part of my life," I said.

"Why does it matter now?" she asked.

I had to tell her. I had wanted to keep my baby-making efforts a secret because I didn't want to add any pressure on the process. I also secretly thought telling her might jinx our attempts. Mom had always joked that the goat kids would be the only grandchildren she would get out of me. But now I had to fess up: Even though I had sworn off having children for a million years, I told her, Bill and I were now trying to conceive. I stumbled over the words, and even as I told her about my plan, I had doubts. When I was done, there was a silence on the other line. "Hello?" I said.

"Oh, Novella!" she gushed. My mom was thrilled. After giving me some conception advice—legs up, feed Bill oysters— she asked when was the next time I was fertile. I hemmed and hawed before changing the subject to her golf game. I didn't want to bring up the fact that I might be impregnated with a demon baby.

My sister called the next day for the dad report. My fear that I was carrying a demon baby had been relieved: That morning I had gotten my period. Now, examined rationally, my premonition seemed dangerously close to one of my dad's paranoid visions. What did I have in mind—a Satan chipmunk baby with goat eyes?

As Riana and I talked, I worked in the garden, tearing up the old wood Bill and I had used to build the raised beds long ago. Time, mushrooms, and ants had started to break the wood down; the screws had fallen out and the beds had split open, like overripe seed pods.

My sister had a squat farm too. She raised chickens and goats on a chunk of unused land in her village in the South of France.

"I caught the nutria in a trap last night," she said. A nutria, a large rodent that had been preying on her chickens.

"I ran up to the bar, to the old guy who I borrowed the trap from," she said. "I said, 'I caught the nutria! Can you come and kill it?'; and he said, 'I'm too old for that—you do it,' and went back to eating his bar nuts."

So she ran down to the garden with a sharp knife and thrust the blade into the trap, and killed it. Not wanting to waste the animal's life, they ate the nutria. She even saved the hide and tanned it. Then used the fur to make Amaya an Indian princess outfit.

"Holy shit," I said. "That's badass." I was in awe of her moxie. Then I remembered that I had done a similar thing a few years before. I killed an opossum once with a shovel. It had killed some of my livestock, and I went berserk, decapitating the predator. That rage.

While we talked, I remembered an entry in my sister's teenage diary: "My sister and I got in a fight last night . . . ," she wrote. "I talked about how I got different things from mom and dad. From both sides I get different things. From my father I get anger, frustration, laziness, and survivalness—for lack of a better word. "Will" to survive. Then I asked if she got the same thing." No wonder my sister and I got in a fight over that one. I've always wanted to pretend that I was nothing like my father, but surely I have inherited some of his tendencies. I majored in biology in college, and years of goat breeding had reinforced what I learned: You are essentially a product of your parents' genetic line. You take on their physical and mental traits.

Riana was getting more and more like Dad. Living in a remote place, gathering wild food, tanning hides. She was also getting into tarot cards and following vision quests. I didn't ask her about her paranormal activities—it just seemed too out there.

I asked if she had ever worried about the crazy genes in our family. That they might have been passed on to Amaya. She told me that she hadn't worried about that. She felt like she and Benji were destined to be together, destined to have Amaya.

Riana met Benji when she was in her thirties. My sister always liked guys from different countries, even in high school, and when she met Benji in Las Vegas, at the Paris Hotel of all places, the attraction was immediate. At the time she was living a fast lifestyle in Los Angeles, where she regularly got Botoxed and had collagen inserted into her lips. Those materialistic years were her form of rebellion against our mom. But standing there on the dance floor of the hotel, dancing with Benji, she knew that he was The One. He would whisk her away, first to Paris, then to the South of France, and she would steadily lose that drive toward the superficial and settle into a new, slow life.

Their meeting did feel fated. In 1970, in a village in the South of France—a few kilometers from where my parents were getting busy conceiving Riana—another couple, Chantal and Patrick LaGarde, were doing the same. Benji's parents. Even Mom, who, remembering Dad, always advised us to "Never meet your husband on vacation," agreed that these two were meant to be together. They eventually moved back to the region where they were both conceived and there they conceived their daughter.

"It took Benji and me a year," she reminded me when I told her I still wasn't pregnant, and that I was feeling ambivalent.

Before signing off, Riana said she had some bad news to share. "I'm having hot flashes."

"What?" I asked.

"It's a sign of menopause," she said flatly. I knew about hot flashes, but I associate them with my mom, not my sister. In addition to the itchy hot feeling, Riana had other early menopause symptoms: joint pain and fatigue.

"Oh, man," I said, "You're too young for that!" She had just turned forty.

"Yup, it's what the French doctors told me," she said before saying good-bye. I threw a chewed-up piece of four-by-four into a pile I was planning to burn. I would turn thirty-eight in two months.

"Monkeeey!!" Bill yelled as he rode up to the farm on his bike a few hours later.

"Hey, dog," I said when he came into the garden. I showed him the work I had done on the farm beds, and as we poked around, talking about what to plant for the fall, I mentioned my sister's condition.

"Peri what?" Bill said.

"Peri-menopause. When you stop making the eggs," I said.

"Well, you know, she's real skinny," Bill said.

"So what?"

"Maybe that's the problem," he said, and squeezed my love handles. Then I realized that he was worried that if my sister's reproductive years were coming to a close now, mine couldn't be so far behind either. I was running out of time.

Newly enlisted, George Carpenter, 1955.

Nine

A few days after talking to my mom on the phone about Dad's violent streak, I got a package in the mail from Mom. It contained old photos of Dad and a military plaque that read "U.S. Army Armed Forces, Sgt. George E. Carpenter. Enlisted 30 May 1955, Honorably released 24 March 1958."

After Grandma Jeanne died, her regular cleaning woman had found the military plaques and photos and, not having Dad's address or contact information, sent them to my mom.

"I don't know why she sent them to me, or who would want these things," my mom wrote in a note to me. *They're for me*, I thought, as I unpacked the box. I silently thanked this woman who cleaned out my grandmother's house—and my mom, for hoarding things that were probably painful for her to see. The military placard had a cartoonish illustration of combat soldiers against a blue background. The soldiers were wearing helmets and backpacks. They were running forward with long guns, with eyes cast forward, hopeful.

The photos were taken in Korea. There was a shot of my dad, looking like a gangly teenager, wearing military gear and shoveling snow on the ground. Another one of a thin, rickety tent that must have been home for him while in Korea. Bleak and cold.

The military paraphernalia reminded me of a strange moment from the summer in Idaho Falls when my dad had come to visit me. He had stayed a second night in the closet. In the morning, we went to the farmer's market. While we eyed the Mormon peaches and baked goods I sensed he was feeling antsy and wanted to leave. I loved going to the market, I enjoyed meeting fellow farmers and being part of the scene, but my dad seemed more and more agitated as we wandered through the stalls. "Look, we gotta go," he finally said and grabbed my elbow. We walked toward a bank parking lot, away from the crowd.

"What's wrong?" I asked, rubbing my elbow.

"It's just that crowds—I can't take it. I have to constantly be on the alert." He pulled his cowboy hat down over his forehead. He sounded—well, crazy. "I have to watch my angle, who can attack, what I would do," he muttered. I had chalked it up to him being a feral guy who spent too much time in the woods communing with nature, so that the sounds and sights of the city, even a small one like Idaho Falls, had been a shock to his system, like Crocodile Dundee in Manhattan. Had something happened to him in the military that made him so cagey? Did he have, like soldiers coming back from Iraq and Afghanistan, post-traumatic stress disorder? PTSD could be repressed, and then get triggered by stress or other circumstances.

. . .

After looking at the photos I headed to my office, which is twelve blocks away from my house, along a gritty corridor of Martin Luther King Jr. Way. Along my walk I passed a highway overpass that had become a homeless encampment. It's locally known as The Jungle because in order to reach the camp you have to first climb a tall chain-link fence then hike up an ivy-shrouded hill. At the top, a thicket of trees offered some privacy from the highway. People post notes on the fence for the residents of The Jungle. One memorable one read, "Jim: Makita is in labor. Go to the hospital." It always smelled like piss and pigeon shit nearby.

I continued walking and passed West Grand Avenue, where the Oakland Veterans Administration is located. It's an outpatient center—a place where veterans of foreign wars go for meds and physicals. Though I passed it every day, I had hardly paid attention to the VA before.

A group of vets hung out in front of the building, waiting for the bus. Many of them used canes or were missing limbs. Across the street from the VA there was a park with benches under a cluster of ponderosa pine trees. There, old and young men played chess and smoked. A man with a shopping cart was yelling threats over and over again. I looked around to see who he was fighting with—his yells were deep and serious sounding. But there was no one there, just his shopping cart and an invisible tormentor. The VA bus idled up to the stop, and I read the motto, written in cursive on the back of the bus: SOME GAVE ALL, ALL GAVE SOME.

I couldn't help but think of Dad. How different was he from the shopping-cart pushers? They scrounged for cans and metal while he scrounged the forest for scrap wood to make his living. I wondered if something had happened to him in Korea.

Later, when I came home from my office, I looked for a journal I remembered keeping during a rough patch in my life when I was homeless myself. I searched through the piles of stuff I keep in the shelf near the fireplace. I found it: a journal with a green cover with an Idaho license plate bolted to the front. A gift from my dad. As I thumbed through the pages, I had a sense of vertigo, of falling, back into a past I didn't want to remember.

I found an entry from a dark night in 1994. I was twenty-two years old, in college, living with eight roommates in a squalid house we called The Cabin. That night I was drunk and sad—another guy had rejected me, told me I was "too intense" for him. I put a butter knife in a dirty oven and waited for it to warm to 350 degrees. This rejection was a pattern; I just didn't know how to act around guys. I remembered that diary entry of my sister: "You hear that girls look for a man who is like their father . . ." What about girls who don't have a father?

When the knife was good and hot, I took my shirt off and carried it out to the back porch. It was a cold night, a chestnut tree was losing its leaves outside. As I held the knife to the flesh on my ribcage, I heard a sizzle and closed my eyes against the pain. In my drunken logic, I figured I would give myself a stigmata like the one Christ had, just under his rib. I was a martyr for lost love. The burn welted up and oozed for weeks. I still have a white scar under my right breast, a reminder from a difficult time.

Things weren't all bad, though. In class I had become fascinated by the natural world, the one that had so drawn me when I was a child. I became a biology major and worked in a lab for an entomologist, keeping his assassin bug breeding program on track. If one of the black beetle-looking bugs bit me, I might lose an arm, the venom from one bite was that potent. I never worried, and kept their cages clean and fed them caterpillars for food. The bugs would pounce on the caterpillars, inject them with poison, and then sip their liquefied innards with their long proboscises.

I had another lab job in the next building over, in the human fertility clinic. I collected oocytes from hamsters, took the brown-bagged samples from shame-faced men, and kept the masturbatory room free of stray pubic hairs and restacked the titty magazines. My boss at the clinic once let me look under the microscope at the sperm. I watched the little guys swim industriously toward the enormous hamster ovum. I wanted a boyfriend desperately. But not just any guy. I found myself drawn to the dark brooding types, the misanthropes.

I finally found one who would have me. He worked at the Lusty Lady strip club as a janitor. He was tall and rail thin, and had tattoos on every inch of his body. My favorite tattoo was a Virgin Mary who lived on his thigh. She was traditional except bees were swarming around her mouth and you could see they inhabited her womb too. The tattoos almost made him seem not human. He was a painter of dark and gothic images, and accordingly wore chunky industrial-looking clogs. Our first date involved going to a morgue in the basement of the science building where I worked. There weren't any bodies that day but we did get to see some human livers. The lab guys next to the morgue were casually dissecting the livers while sipping Cokes.

From there, things didn't go well. He was definitely not into normal and healthy. I lost my virginity to him, and rode my bike home the day after, across the Lake Union Bridge, in agony, but feeling victorious. We continued dating for a few months but I usually found myself lying in his cold bed feeling empty and lonely.

It was during this period that I gave myself the stigmata; I dropped out of college soon after. I was twenty-two and found myself living in a van. I cooked meals on a Coleman stove, took sponge baths in the back of the van, and scrawled in my journal, trying to figure out what to do with my life.

In my living room in Oakland, I continued to read from the journal I kept during those dark days. "Riana told Mom I act like Dad now," I read. "Which fascinates me. Maybe I should drive to Idaho? Tomorrow I'm going to get Dad's phone number and call. Oh, man, I'm excited about the adventure I'm going to have!"

I had to laugh when I read that. I've been trying to get my dad's phone number my whole life.

Shortly after I wrote that entry, I had my accident.

I had migrated to Portland and was working as a dishwasher by then. One night, riding my bike home from the restaurant, a piece of tenderloin beef stolen from the restaurant's walk-in tucked into my pants, I ran a stop sign. A car did the same, and clipped my back tire, sending the bike scrapping sideways across the street, my left leg caught up under the heavy metal frame. The boozy-smelling driver silently handed me a cigarette as we examined my mangled Raleigh three-speed. I stood, flamingo-like, on my right leg—my left leg hung off to the side and felt numb.

A few days after my accident, thinking that my foot would heal in a matter of weeks, I jumped in a van with some hippies I had been living with in Portland. They were going to New York City, and I invited myself along. I propped myself in the back of their VW bus, and, as the states blurred by, I watched my foot turn from red to purple to a faint yellow by the time we got to New York. My plan was to stay with a friend of a friend in Brooklyn; he had a studio apartment in Carroll Gardens. He let me stay for a few weeks, but after that I had to leave, and I found myself homeless and still limping from the accident. I was trapped in the city, penniless. I spent nights riding the subway, scratching at the dirt on my skin, which came off in coils. One night a guy sat across from me, and when I looked up he was pulling at this giant plastic thing and making guttural sounds. I realized the plastic thing was his dick. The masturbator stared at me, and instead of fear, a hot rage trickled down into my heart. I went berserk, attacked him, kicking and hitting him until he fled the subway car—I wanted to kill him with my bare hands.

Meanwhile I wrote letters to friends, never mentioning my problems, keeping it breezy and romantic sounding. Now that I thought of it, they were akin to my dad's postcards to me. I hoped someone might read between the lines and figure out that I needed saving.

As I browsed through my journal, I saw the photo. It's a self-portrait, taken on the bed of a cockroach-infested SRO in Harlem. By then I had found a job dishwashing for $4 an hour. The long days spent standing were killing my injured foot, but I had to pay for the SRO. I ate the food that came back to me in the dishwashing galley, but it was never enough. In the photo I look gaunt and scared. In another, there's a double exposure taken of me with the city behind me. Around my neck are a pair of dog tags. I don't remember how or where I got them, but they hung from a metal chain and I would finger the braille-like name and number: Carpenter, George, RA2877979715 T56.

I slammed the journal closed, feeling shaky and disoriented. Maybe my dad was right; maybe I *had* torn into him like a cur dog: a dog seeing its own reflection.

Eventually I got bailed out of New York by a friend, my college roommate. She happened to be driving to Cornell and offered to pick me up in upstate New York. When we met up in Poughkeepsie I was a mess; I had a limp, my clothes were filthy, and I clutched my army/navy store rucksack like a life preserver. She drove me to her mom's house in St. Paul, who took pity on me and had me do odd jobs until I earned enough money to get home to Seattle.

Once I was back in Seattle, my mom loaned me some money, and I found a real house to live in. I went back to college and finished up.

Then, when I was twenty-five, I met Bill.

Bill seemed to love my faults. At his Capitol Hill apartment, he dumpster-dived for food and discarded objects that were broken but beautiful to him. He told me he liked my crooked teeth, my greasy hair, my tattered clothing, the white stigmata scar. My intensity was met by his intractable calmness, like a hot knife placed in cool water. I often felt like one of the things he had fished out of the junk piles. In turn, I was attracted to his somewhat uncivilized behaviors, like blowing his nose with a tube sock, wearing ripped jeans, and keeping a crazy head of hair. My story has a happy ending. I finally met someone who loved me, and that love made everything seem possible.

I put the journal away and stared out at the garden. I felt like I had just time traveled. I could only vaguely remember what my life was like back then. That past self was a stranger to me—a young woman having a hard time, and yet not really upset about it. Just surviving, like my dad.

Based on what I had seen in Orofino, Dad was putting on a brave face, but he was in desperate straits, just like I had been in New York. He clearly needed help now. But there was no one to help him. Just me.

I was the only one who knew how bad things had gotten for him. I wasn't scared of his violent temper: I had one to match his. Maybe I could return to Orofino and help make some improvements to his cabin. Together we could clean up his house. Dig a new outhouse. Set up a rain catchment system. I was his daughter—maybe I could help mend what his friend John called his "broken fences."

But it was more than just wanting to help. I also wanted to finally break out of our pattern. I felt like I could control our destiny, to change our way of being toward each other. I sent him an apology and proposed that we get together as soon as possible—in October or November.

The next day, my father had already replied to my e-mail that I should come back, he would be ready for me. I booked my plane ticket for the end of October.

I was going back to Orofino.

PART III

—

FOUND

The Rough House: half-built in 1973
and, finally, finished, 1976.

Ten

I drove into Orofino, past the Pink House Hole where Bill and I had camped for a few days back in August. The Idaho air felt different; it was saturated with water, and the broadleaf trees had turned yellow amid a delirium of evergreen. The river was swollen and moved faster than it had in the summer. As I drove over the bridge and passed the Ponderosa Café, I got that "coming home" feeling. A fullness in my stomach and chest. A slight flutter of panic—a feeling of drowning. What am I doing here?

On this trip to Orofino, Bill hadn't come with me. He was on goat birth watch—the does were due any day. I missed him. But I did have the help and support of some of the happy hippies from Farm Out. Lowell, Phil, and Tom had recently met up and decided they wanted to help me on my "dad quest," as they were calling it. It was decided that Tom, my mom's ex-boyfriend, would pick me up at the Lewiston airport and let me borrow his car to drive to Orofino. Lowell and Phil cleared out the little hand-built cabin on Farm Out so I would have a place to stay. Phil sent me a couple more stories he remembered from the old days that might give me some perspective about my dad.

The only problem was my dad wouldn't be there. Two days before my flight was due to leave for Idaho, he had sent me an e-mail:

hi sweets, heading to Az this am, will contact when settled.
best love always, pops

Stunned, I reread his message. He knew I was coming to see him, and he was leaving. I had all these do-gooder notions about how I was going to help my old, broken dad out. But now that he was blowing me off—yet another time—it triggered a wave of anger that I realized had always floated deep down in me. Fuck him, I said out loud.

Later that day, I called my mom to tell her that Dad had left Idaho.

"Can you get your money back for the plane ticket?" she had asked, ever the pragmatist.

"Oh, I'm still going," I said.

She sounded shocked. "Why?"

I felt the familiar red-hot anger. "He's going to find out that you can't just make someone—there are consequences."

"Watch the drama," she advised, and I remembered her story about wanting to burn down the house.

I deplaned at the Lewiston airport, forty-seven miles east of Orofino, and was greeted by Tom—and his wife Judy. Tom's hair had gone completely white. His eyes were warm and brown, and when he smiled, it revealed his gap tooth. His teeth looked healthy and white—surprising to me because he had never used a toothbrush when he and my mom had been together. A ban on toothbrushes and toothpaste were one of his hippie tics. There were others: a deep hatred of Comet cleaning powder, insisting on only using cast iron pans for cooking. Looking back on these quirks, I find them funny, but I realize I have plenty of my own. Like insisting on using a car that runs on fuel made from vegetable oil, or my own ban on using underarm deodorant.

Mom and Tom broke up over one of these lifestyle choices.

When I was in high school, Mom and Tom almost bought a house together in Moscow, Idaho. Tom was my mom's future for after Riana and I left her for college. But things fell apart, apparently over my mom's request to get a dishwasher for the new house. Tom felt that dishes should be washed by hand, using Dr. Bronner's soap—and not cleaned by a soul-robbing machine. They ended up not moving in together, and broke up. Maybe the dishwasher was a symbol for Tom, of living an idealistic life, having unwavering ideals, never selling out. Tom, like my dad, had a code that he wanted to live by. My mom is similarly uncompromising. Of course they were doomed.

Instead of moving in with Tom in Idaho, my mom stayed in her house in Shelton, and Riana and I left the nest my mom had built for us. We took off without looking back or thinking about how she would be affected by our sudden absence. The only clue I had that my mom was heartbroken was a letter she stuffed into the moving boxes that I took with me to college. Her letter to me detailed my strengths and weaknesses—and her hopes for me. It ended by telling me that she found herself crying, for no reason, in the middle of the day. I read the letter in my dorm room, boxes half-unpacked, and then went out to dinner with my new dorm mate, and didn't think about it again.

After Mom and Tom broke up, Tom met Judy, a nice Christian lady, and married her. I was scandalized. My mom was resigned, and she told me that people go back to what they knew—Tom had been raised by a religious family. Mom said she was tired of the emotional turmoil of having a boy-friend, anyway. She was fifty years old when they split, and hasn't dated anyone since.

At Tom and Judy's house, where I would stay the night before driving to Orofino the next day, I sniffed for the smells I associated with Tom: peppermint Dr. Bronner's, sandal-wood. I looked for batik fabric and African statues. Nothing. As I looked around, I noticed that I felt sad. Seeing Tom pained me. He had been like a rare treasure—a good, gentle man—that my mom had lost. I also noticed that Tom and Judy had a dishwasher.

I borrowed Tom's car and drove to Orofino. I crossed the bridge and headed to the IGA. I called Bill. He was riding his bike to work.

"I'm at the IGA," I told him.

"How's it going?" he asked.

"I don't know, I feel sad," I said.

"It's OK, dog," he said. God, I love him.

Later I found myself unpacking my stuff into Phil's cabin on Lowell's property. The cabin was shrouded by a glade of pine trees that must have been saplings when the place was built. I loved the angles of cabin, the way the windows were made with salvaged glass. The rocking chair next to the potbellied woodstove. The front porch with its slanted roof. It looked like a gold-miner's cabin. Phil, an English professor at the University of Idaho, had told me he had hoped it would be a place where he would get lots of writing done. As I surveyed the cabin, I felt like I was a visitor from the future who had stepped back into history. I didn't belong, but I did. I had been here before.

Down the road from the cabin, in the big house, Lowell seemed harried but happy. He was unloading wood from a truck to stack up for the winter. Upstairs his two teenaged daughters were making dinner. Dark-haired and giggly, they seemed curious about why I, this younger friend of their dad's, had come back again. But they were too shy to ask.

"Should we make potatoes too?" Lowell asked when he came upstairs. His daughters and I went out to the garden. It was just starting to fade—a few cabbages, the last of the summer zucchini. Red apples glowed from a tree in the corner of the garden. Lowell sunk his pitchfork into a pile of dirt surrounded with yellow leaves and stems and turned the soil. Yellow and red potatoes popped out of the dark earth. His younger daughter and I scrambled after them, dusted them off, and put them into a bucket. Then we walked through the stand of sweet corn and picked ten ears. Lowell threw some pigweed to the fattening pigs. The girls obviously worshiped their dad.

I wondered what it would have been like if my parents had been happy together on the ranch. I imagined this idyllic life growing up on the land—like Lowell's girls, I would have gone to Orofino High, raised pigs for 4-H, ridden horses. I got a strange sense of vertigo considering this parallel universe.

After dinner the girls wandered off to study and talk on the phone, and Lowell showed me a photo of the rig he and his first wife Marcia used to drive down to Arizona. It was a camper that fit on a flatbed truck, like a little cabin.

They looked so young and blond, and free. Lowell sighed. "I don't like looking at these," he said.

"Why not?" I asked. I got a thrill looking at old photos from back in the happy hippie days.

"Marcia made this album," he said, "I don't like old photos because I don't like to be reminded about how young I was. It's evidence of my decline."

"But you're in great shape," I said.

"That's why I stayed here, on this land, so my body could stay strong," he said. "But it's still not as strong as it was before."

I knew what he was talking about—I hadn't thought about it before, but I was in my prime right now. My farm work—milking the goats, throwing bales of alfalfa, working the garden—kept me strong and healthy. Something I had taken for granted. I hadn't thought about the day when everything wasn't possible, when I would feel weak and tired.

That night, curled up in front of the potbellied stove in Phil's cabin, I went over my plan. I had decided, over the last few days, that I wanted to have a few moments inside my dad's house. If I couldn't make contact with the man, at least I could examine his den. I especially wanted to read the card I recognized as my own, stuck to his wall. Why did he save that one? I also wanted to look through the closets and unearth some knowledge of him. Even if I didn't find anything tangible, I wanted to go inside and sit there for a while. To get into his skin.

The next morning I woke up to the sound of Maya's black

horse thundering past the cabin, snorting. It was cold and drizzly. I made a nest of twigs and newspaper in the stove and lit it. I thought of old friends of mine who I hadn't seen in a while, and wondered if I would feel the pang of years gone by like Lowell. Then I bundled up and walked to Lowell's house. We drank coffee, both dreading what we were going to do that day. Lowell went to his divorce hearing. I went to my dad's cabin.

I drove into town, then turned up Grangemont Road, where my father lived. I felt sick but mesmerized, unable to stop myself from going to his place. I had an instinctual need, almost a thirst to go back to his cabin, to see it without the distraction of him being there.

The forest along the road was dismal and gray in October, and it closed in as I got closer to his place. When I drove up to the gravel driveway, a thin rain began to fall. The house looked bleak and empty. His truck wasn't there. I was surprised to see there were some piles of firewood left—maybe a stockpile in case Arizona didn't work out? Or maybe he just hadn't sold all the wood he had gathered that season, or it wasn't fully dry and needed to cure for longer. A little gray kitten—one of a whole litter—darted out from under the cabin. In the path to the porch I saw a chipmunk tail, just the fur left, from the kittens' hunting.

"Dad?" I called and knocked on the door. I tried turning the doorknob, but it wouldn't budge. In the hollow below, someone was playing music, old hits from the 1950s like The Supremes and Elvis. The music drifted up, which added a strange cinematic soundtrack.

I circled around the side of the house, looking for openings in the windows. At the back door, there were some tossed food scraps, half of a red pepper, bright against the dark soil of the woods, and some bread that didn't look moldy. This midden made me think he had left more recently than I had thought. There was a ladder, which I picked up and placed on the side of the back door. I felt wounded, half-crazy. As I climbed the ladder, I heard voices. I froze, clutching the rungs.

"Do you like squash?" a woman's voice said. "Squash . . . ?" a wavering old man's voice queried.

"Winter squash. Because we grew some big ones—like twenty-pounders!" the woman bragged. Though they sounded like they were right outside my dad's cabin, their voices were actually from below, where the music was coming from. I relaxed.

"Oh!" the man chortled, "Isn't that nice?"

"I'll. Bring. You. Some. We're. Sharing. With the Neighbors," the woman enunciated so he would understand. I stopped listening and went back to figuring out the puzzle of how to get in. There was no way I wasn't going in, I thought. No way. When I get an idea in my head like this one, I become focused and unrelenting, like a pit bull. I went back around to the front of the cabin and stood at the door.

This whole thing—our relationship—felt like a manhunt. I would make an effort to see him, then give up. I was sick of playing, and I wanted to finally make a breakthrough with him so I could move on. But every time, he had eluded me. Now, I had come all this way, and I wanted to get what I had come for; I didn't want to be skunked again. I felt a surge of energy and raised up my leg and began kicking. Wood from the door started to buckle and chip. With one last push with my shoulder, the door creaked open, and the two-by-fours holding the door shut fell away.

"Hello?" I called, stepping over the pieces of wood my dad

had used to secure the door. Kittens scattered as I walked up the wobbly interior stairs. Then I was inside. The place smelled musty and rank. A cup of coffee sat on the counter—it had mold growing on the top. Maybe he had been gone longer than I thought.

I noticed I was breathing hard, not just from the effort of breaking in, but from fear. I had a horrible sensation that my dad would drive up, and I would be there, caught. So I worked quickly, starting with the card that I had seen during the last visit. It was green construction paper and had a tree with sparkles hand-drawn on it. It was from about 1994, when I was still in college. It was a full report of my grades from my classes at the University of Washington. "I got a 3.2 in chemistry, 3.6 in English. Pretty good, though I'm wondering if this is just a rat race—what does it all mean?" I had dropped out shortly after, and began my free fall.

After I pinned the card back up on the wall, I moved to the back of the cabin where I opened up all the drawers and cupboards. The newspaper clippings of the wedding photos from the Clearwater Tribune caught my eye again. When I had initially seen these clippings, I assumed Dad knew these people, but now I was almost positive these people were strangers to him. It was as if he had wanted to have some clippings from the past, but he wasn't organized enough to keep any photos. So he had used these clippings as surrogates.

The file cabinet held all the books that he cared about—*The Sun Also Rises*, *The Great Gatsby*, and other classics. The cupboards had weird stuff like Seal-a-Meal packets and emergency flares. In the kitchen I found empty bottles of the medication he was taking: atorvastatin, hydrochlorothiazide, and amitriptyline. These felt like clues in a treasure hunt: he wouldn't tell me about his health but I could find out what kind of maladies I—and my future children—might suffer from via these medications. I wrote the names of the meds in a notebook so I could research them later.

There was an open book on his table entitled *How to Write Screenplays*. A closet door, opened, revealed a few shotguns, rain gear, and tools. Then, when I was just starting to feel almost nauseous with panic that I was violating my dad's privacy, I found the gold: a notebook on the end table by the couch. Feeling sick, I stood by the window and read it, gulping down every detail like a starving dog. The phone number for a man who wanted wood, a message in Spanish that he had sent to me while I was in Idaho Falls, his social security number, John Garrick's address, and personal thoughts and revelations that he had had. One was a question: "What are you after you've lost everything you loved?" And another, almost a haiku, about my mom: "Pat: a terribly wonderful mother; a wonderfully terrible wife."

These last two entries were written on the last pages of the notebook. Written recently, I wondered if my visit had released these troubling thoughts.

Before I left the cabin, I sat in his hard chair and felt dreadful. His lonely life enveloped me. "This is how it feels to be my dad," I muttered. I took a deep breath. The view from the front window was trees and overgrown bracken. The floor beneath me felt rough, uneven. This was the life he had carved out of the woods. He hadn't compromised—but this is what he had left, a lonely, cold cabin.

And even this cabin, this almost-unlivable structure, would not be passed on to me. Inside the notebook I also found a letter. It was written to Dad on embossed paper, from the University of California, San Francisco. Dad had, in the early eighties, gone back to college to earn his degree. He only had a few semesters left, and so he moved to San Francisco and reenrolled into the UC system. The letter was some paperwork for granting his estate to the university once he died. Dad hadn't filled it out, but it was clear: this cabin, the one semi-valuable thing he had left, would be going to UCSF, not to me or my sister. For a beat I was appalled and hurt. Then I started chuckling, imagining the UCSF endowment agent visiting this shack.

I stood up and walked out the sliding door. At the front door, shards of two-by-four hung from the doorway. This was going to be tough to explain, I thought. Maybe he would think a bear tried to break in? I jammed the door closed as best I could.

I paused as I walked by the small vegetable patch. Things were still growing nicely, despite the cold. There were some peas, and the tomatoes were still bearing some red fruit. I picked a few tomatoes and a pair of acorn squashes to take back to Lowell's. The zucchini plant was still blooming. During our visit, whenever Dad had passed by the zucchini plant, its orange flowers yawning open, he would shout, "Goddamn, that is a beautiful!" with an extreme and heartfelt zeal. It came from the same place as his repulsion for clear-cuts, the one that made him fall to his knees and cry, "This is a desecration!" He felt things—good and bad—so intensely.

I didn't know it then, but someone had been watching me, shotgun aimed at my head, while they waited for the police to come. As I backed the car out of my dad's driveway, the acorn squash rolling around on the passenger seat, I saw a police car drive up, followed by a big SUV with lights mounted on top. I paused in my backing up to let them pass until I realized they had come for me.

For a moment, I considered running. I could make it into the dense forest in just a few seconds. Instead, I took a deep breath and rolled down my window, car still idling, looking confused at the tall woman police officer. Can't a daughter break into her dad's cabin? Apparently no. I had forgotten where I was—not in a city where I was used to being anonymous. In the woods, the hills have eyes.

"Ma'am, is this your car?" she asked.

"Um, no, it's a friend's," I answered. I got out of the car, realizing I might be in big trouble. I felt the same sensation of dread when I had been caught trying to burn down the apartment building when I was twelve. I was conscious of how I looked—wearing a wool sweater and a dirty down vest, hair wild. My heart was sick from what I had done and what I had seen. Instead of doing a judo chop, or running away into the woods, which is what I desperately wanted to do, I handed the police my driver's license.

Then I noticed a man, my dad's neighbor, leaning against his gun, watching the whole thing unfold. He was lanky with curly gray hair; the gun was made of blond wood.

"So why are you here?" the female cop asked. "Does your dad know you are here?"

"Yeah, he knows I'm in Orofino. I just thought he might still be here. I wanted to check on him." I started to choke up. "I'm worried about him. I think he might not be doing well. You know, he's old," I started rambling.

"I think I talked to you last year," the woman cop said.

She turned out to be the young officer, the one I talked to when my dad went missing.

Thank god, this cop and I practically knew each other! I'm not sure what I was worried about—that I'd be arrested for breaking and entering? That they'd tell my dad?

One of the guy cops, a mustached man in a baseball cap, walked down to the cabin to check out the door. He whispered something to her when he came back.

"I've been meaning to talk to you guys," I said, sniffling. "I wanted to find out why you thought he was missing."

The neighbor with the gun, who was waiting in the wings, watching the whole thing go down, approached. "He left his guitar on the couch," the neighbor said, "so I called the police." The pesky neighbor suddenly seemed kind of sweet.

"Well, we knew he had his secret spots to go find logs, so we had to go everywhere looking for him," the mustached officer said.

"You were on the manhunt?" I asked.

"Yep, your dad has a lot of secret places," he said, with obvious pride at my seventy-four-year-old woodsman father. I grinned.

After they ran my driver's license and I checked out without a record, the cops shook my hand. "Nice to meet you!" I said to them, relieved. I would have been busted if I hadn't been his daughter. Of course, I wouldn't have been there if I hadn't been his daughter.

The police vehicles backed up and left. I felt almost giddy, like I had gotten away with something. In Native American tradition, there is the idea of counting coup—of touching the enemy to let them know you could have done damage but were peaceful. I had just counted coup on my dad.

. . .

A few hours after breaking into Dad's cabin, Lowell and I sat in his kitchen, eating chips and drinking beer. He had an amazing collection of beer cozies.

"So was your dad there?" Lowell asked.

"No," I answered.

I told Lowell about breaking in, getting caught, and then the strange encounter I had with the neighbor—after the cops left, the neighbor invited me into his house for tea.

The neighbor and his wife sat and talked with me about my dad, who had been living across the road from them for the past thirteen years. Their house was beautiful. It was hand built—the beams were made of whole logs, the wooden floors gleamed golden. His wife was frosting a cake when we came in.

"This is George Carpenter's daughter," he told her.

"Oh—George," she said, smiling. "We watch out for him."

"Thank you," I said, then immediately broke into tears.

We sat down for tea, and they told me what they knew. He had been on a routine for years. At 7:30 a.m. he leaves for town, where he goes to the post office, then plays a few games of pool, then goes to the library.

"But something's been up," the neighbor said. "He's been acting weird the last year or so." Like leaving so early for Arizona. "He usually goes late October, November."

I said it was my fault, that I had been hounding him.

He told me that in 2001, things with my dad had gotten really bad. He started acting really weird and antisocial—he even threatened to kill their dog. Then, that summer, he disappeared for a few months.

"I think he got some medical help," she said.

"Listen, kid, your dad's a survivor. He's barely holding on—he doesn't have anything to give you," the neighbor said, rocking in his chair. I nodded.

While I told Lowell the story, I felt a yearning sensation, I guess sympathy, for my dad. He was empty, a shell of a man. Maybe if I had made an effort to connect with him sooner, things would have been different. I realized that our last time together—our last real time—was spent on the banks of Ririe; me learning how to cast, him trying to connect. But I'd lost him, I had arrived too late.

After dinner with Lowell, I headed back to my cabin, exhausted. The mist came down as I walked the dark road. I stoked the fire in the stove and pulled out my journal. I was almost thirty-eight, and for the first time I felt like an adult. I wrote in my journal that night, "It's so strange, I came here to find my dad but I'm finding myself instead."

Before I went to sleep, I checked my e-mail, which had been coming in sporadically in Idaho. There was a message from my dad, sent that afternoon:

> *Hi sweets, returning to Idaho to regroup; saw John Garrick*
> *on my way back; keep me posted. Love papa.*

I went numb in the legs with fear. He's back from Arizona so soon? I'll actually see him? There was no chance he wouldn't notice the door I had kicked in, and now I wouldn't be able to blame a bear or a marauding teenager like I had hoped. And his neighbor would no doubt tell him what I did. This was getting really fucked up.

I called Bill in a panic and told him the whole story.

"Whoa," he said.

"And now how do I explain the break-in?"

Bill, ever the pragmatist, said, "Just tell him you needed to take a nap."

The next day I awoke to the dark cabin. I had moved downstairs in the middle of the night in order to sleep next to the warm stove. It was raining outside and the cabin was freezing.

I drove into town, ate at the Ponderosa Café. A man sat at the counter with a nickel and a bunch of lottery tickets. "Oh, we do this every day," he explained. Scratch cards. "Someday we're going to win!" the waitress said. "One time we won one hundred and fifty dollars. Course we spent that on more tickets." When I walked out of the café I worried that Dad might be at the pool hall down the street, and he would see me. I scurried toward my car.

"Hello?" a woman's voice called. I looked up to see my dad's neighbor's wife on the sidewalk. "That was fun yesterday," she said, and waved. I waved back and nodded. This town was becoming like a group therapy session.

I decided that on my last day in Orofino, I had to go up to the ranch, my childhood home. Though the house was gone, the land still held some spell over me.

It was with a mixture of fear and curiosity that I drove out there, remembering the bends in the road, the wild apple trees swaying with red fruit. Thimbleberries and ponderosa pines. I felt uneasy. I drove past Max's house, around the pasture that he hoped to turn into a peach orchard, and onto the back one hundred acres where the Rough House had been. As I drove, I was surprised to see that street signs had sprung up. In a spot that I remembered as deep forest where we would pick sprays of Indian paintbrush in the spring, there was an official-looking blue-and-white sign and a house at the end of a paved driveway. There were power lines. Not quite the suburbs, but the land felt more populated than it had once been.

At the straightaway where the road ended, where the trailer used to be, was a rustic-looking cabin. The car rumbled over the cattle guard as I drove toward the site where the Rough House used to sit. At the gate hung a FOR SALE sign. Where the apple orchard had been, there was a new house with a large porch and a steeply pitched roof. Greenhouses and garages sat near where the Rough House had been.

The view off toward Orofino was the same—desolate rolling hills, small craggy mountains, and pine trees. I got out of the car and walked up to the new house. The woman who answered the door was doing laundry and wore a robe. "I used to live here," I told her. "Well, I mean, not here, but on this land." She raised her eyebrows, pulled the robe tighter around her body, and crossed her arms.

"Call the number on the sign," she said and shut the door. So much for rural friendliness. Maybe she had discovered the evil spirits on this land. I wrote down the number for the real estate agent, looked around one more time, and drove off in a puff of dust.

I wanted to somehow hold on to the place, to take some of it with me, but I didn't know how to do it.

Back at the entrance to the property, just past Max's house, I pulled over to a glade created where a few back roads converged. One road led back to town, another was an old logging road that was a shortcut to the highway to Lewiston. I dialed the real estate agent and left a message about the house. I said I was a Californian looking to acquire a ranch in Idaho. I was clinging to anything. I wanted someone to talk to. My phone rang. It was my sister, Riana. It's uncanny: she always knows when to call me, when I'm feeling sad or in trouble.

"Hey, Riana, guess where I am?" I asked.

"Idaho?"

"Yeah, I'm at the gate to the ranch!" I got out of the car and sat on the hood. I gave her a report about what I saw and how different the ranch looked. While I talked, I noticed the glade was full of Woods' roses. The bushes had bloomed in May and were now bursting with orange rosehips. I fished an old plastic water bottle out of the back of the car and I started picking.

"I broke into Dad's cabin," I confessed.

"No way!"

I told her the whole sordid story, about what I had found there, about the cops, and the neighbor.

"Dad's going to be pissed," I said, and told her that he was back in Orofino. I had so violated his privacy. As I talked to her, I saw an old guy in a blue truck drive by and pull over. Distracted, I figured he was the property owner of this glade, and didn't want me to pick the rose hips.

"Just a minute, Riana," I said, walking toward the truck. "I think this guy wants to tell me something."

The guy hung his head out of the truck window. He had a funny look on his face. I realized: It was Dad.

I yelled into the phone, "Riana—it's Dad!" I handed the phone to him.

"This is like an acid trip," Dad said into the phone. "I have just had the most unbelievable seven days," he told her, while looking me. His eyes were clear and bright. "I've seen everyone and every place that I loved. And now this—little

Novella here at the ranch, talking to you on the phone!" He seemed winded, like it was taking a lot out of him.

He handed me the phone. "I'll talk to you later, OK, Riana?" I said.

Dad got out of his truck and we hugged. We walked over to where I had parked my car.

"You could write this as a film and people wouldn't believe it," Dad yelled. His voice echoed through the valley. He was right. The whole shit storm had come full circle to end right here at the ranch where it began.

He had already cried today, he told me, because he had been listening to a show on NPR in the truck about post-traumatic stress disorder. He thought he had it, from Korea. The war was officially over when he was there, but he still had been deployed as a gunner, dropped behind enemy lines, where he marched for miles and miles, sleeping in the snow. "It was brutal," he whistled. "So cold, so unbearable. They say not everyone gets it," he said. "But the ones most likely to come from families with no support structure. Like me." I remembered his mom—ghostlike, barely alive, in her hospital bed. PTSD causes recurrent dreams of violence, social withdrawal. It makes having intimate relationships difficult.

I nodded.

He said it can spring up later, many years after the event that caused it. "We push it back, we don't think about it. And then one day, it all comes blowing out. That's what happened to me. I remember, I was clearing some land on the ranch—you were just a baby—and I was standing on a hill, and maybe a plane went by, and I just lost it. I went back into my mode. That was the first time." He began to weep, and I hugged him.

"It's OK, it's OK," I said, like I was comforting a child.

He pulled away and stood on an old stump. I sat on the hood of the car. I suddenly felt exhausted. Thirty-seven years later, we had collided here.

He seemed so happy to see me. I wondered why he wasn't pissed about my trespassing. "I'm sorry that I went into your house," I said.

"You mean the one that burned down?" he looked confused. Then I realized he hadn't been home yet, he was literally just arriving back to Idaho.

"No, the one where you live," I confessed.

"What are you looking for?" he asked me. His brown eyes searched mine. It was the first time he had ever asked me a question about myself.

"I want to heal myself," I told him. "And," I said, sobbing, "I want someone to blame."

"I'm empty, babes," he said, and spread his hands out, then leaned against a tree. "I'm empty." And he wept.

"I have been so angry and unreasonable," he said. "I've been a terror and a madman. But I'm not doing any harm now." He hocked a loogie.

"In 2001, I was going to blow my brains out," he said. "So I checked into the loony bin. Those twenty-three days in Seattle, talking it out with other soldiers, helped me."

Then the moment was over. I walked him back to his truck, hugged him, forgiving him as I did so. He pulled away, headed back to his cabin. I sat in the glade for a while, just breathing and thinking about what happened. Little Novella. My dad still thought of me as a small child. A mythological white-haired little girl there in that glade.

The next day I would see Dad one more time. He didn't

mention our intense reunion. It seemed like he didn't remember it at all. He also didn't mention the mangled door to his cabin. Instead he told me a story about a guy he knew in Arizona. The man was eighty years old and he could still play tennis every day. I nodded, agreed that keeping fit was important.

A pause in the conversation came, and I cast around for how to tell him about my plan to get pregnant. I just didn't know what to say.

"There's an old guy in Arizona," Dad started again. "He's eighty, and he plays tennis every day." I looked at him, searching his brown eyes. Did he know he was repeating himself? His eyes were bright with excitement, fresh with the tidbit he had just delivered. He wasn't remembering things. It didn't even matter if I told him. He was hollowed out.

That night I drove to Lewiston and returned Tom's car. He took me to the airport. He stayed with me until my flight left. I told him about my encounter with Dad, and his fading mental state.

Tom's eyes widened when I told him about breaking into Dad's cabin. He probably thought that I was being a crazy bitch. And to some extent, I was. I had felt so wounded for all these years. To finally lash out, to attack, was crazy, but it felt right, it felt authentic.

As we talked, I felt a sense of accomplishment. I had done the work I had needed to do. The past I had explored and dredged up was over. Sifting through it, element by element, helped me finally let it settle.

There was also something unexpected: seeing my dad and

breaking into his cabin had made me feel powerful. I didn't share that sensation of power with Tom. He, like my dad, and like Lowell, Phil, Mom, and all the characters in my past, were growing weaker; they were diminishing and shrinking. I was the strong one left standing; I had the future to look forward to. This new knowledge made me giddy—I was the next generation—but it also made me feel a little scared too, with the responsibility it carries.

My mom's grandkid, a young goat
at Ghost Town Farm, 2010.

Eleven

When I returned to Oakland, I told the story of my reunion with Dad to everyone: to my sister, my mother, to Bill, to friends, trying to make sense of it. Riana thought it was somehow destiny, part of the prearranged path of our relationship. My mom declared that he was faking it, that he never showed any symptoms of PTSD when they were together, and he was just trying to blame the war for his own character faults. I looked up the medications he was taking. One for high blood pressure, one for the heart, and an antipsychotic. I'll never know if his problems stemmed from abandonment, military service, or an aberrant gene. Whatever it was that was haunting him, I had moved on.

Having a baby suddenly gave me clarity of purpose. It was Bill and my chance to create something new and fresh out of so much damage. Maybe it was reckless—knowing what I knew about my genetic makeup—but I had come to the understanding that I am a reckless person. Baby-making ensued with a reborn sense of urgency.

"What's that big thing in Mexico?" Bill asked one morning, after a torrid night of baby-making, apropos of nothing.

"A sombrero?" I guessed.

"No," Bill said, offering no more hints.

"A papaya?"

"Yeah! Let's eat one of those tomorrow." Then he wandered off, back to the bathtub, his favorite place of refuge before a long afternoon and evening wrenching cars. He hates mornings and often sleeps in a hot bath before heading to work around one. Then he takes another hot bath after work.

I padded into the kitchen, made some herbal tea, and sat down to my computer. I wondered if my ambivalence was preventing me from getting pregnant. Why was I still not knocked up? It was December 2010; we had been trying for over a year. I had started to question Bill's fertility. "Have you *ever* gotten anyone pregnant," I accused him one night over dinner. Bill had shrugged. "Not that I know of." He wasn't sweating it. He was enjoying his duties as procreator.

So it was finally down to this: I went to a baby website and clicked on the Tips for Getting Pregnant tab. Glancing through advice to avoid coffee and cigarettes, I thought, *didn't everyone know this already?* Then I read the Get Him Ready, Too section, which I hadn't researched yet. It said, "Men should make sure that their testes are not too hot as this can kill sperm. They should avoid hot baths, tight-fitting underwear and jeans, and using a portable computer balanced on the lap as all these things raise scrotal temperature."

My glasses fogged up when I burst into the bathroom. Bill was dozing peacefully, his head buoyed by a blow-up neck pillow. I perched my glasses on my head and surveyed naked Billy. He was almost completely submerged, the water licked the top of the tub, a few rivulets escaped when he sleepily shifted to fold his hands across his belly.

I cleared the books and newspapers off the toilet and sat down. Billy started to snore. The family jewels were floating in the hot bathwater, looking like fish balls in my favorite Cambodian soup. I stuck a finger in the water. Almost scalding. I let out a sigh. Survival of the fittest, I mumbled.

After troubleshooting the hot bath problem, I approached getting pregnant like my father had approached a log-clearing job, with a burning intensity. I scoured as many baby-making websites for secret tips to boost fertility as I could. I drastically changed my diet—I began sipping nettle tea, eating whole grains, no Chinese takeout—to nurture my womb. I jumped on Bill like a crazy monkey when I knew I was ovulating. I also turned to needles. Acupuncture needles.

There's a Chinese Medicine place near my office in downtown Oakland, and a friend suggested that I go there. When I walked in, the clinic smelled of moxibustion smoke and herbs. At a little desk on the third floor, the receptionist smiled up at me.

I looked around, suddenly feeling skittish. "I want to get acupuncture to get pregnant," I blurted. I hate going to the doctor—the vulnerability of being sick or broken often overwhelms me, and even during a routine exam, I tend to cry.

She nodded and handed me some forms to fill out. I was relieved that they weren't standard hospital questions about my medical history; the Chinese doctors simply wanted to

know if my hands were cold, how many times a day I uri-
nated, and how many hours of sleep did I get at night.

Then I was shown into a room painted light green with
white trim. There was an examination bed, covered with
paper, in the middle of the room. A student doctor went over
my records. Then a tiny woman named Dr. Ye came into the
room, wearing a pink scarf. She sat down across from me and
had me stick out my tongue. She had gentle brown eyes, but
she furrowed her eyebrows when she felt my pulse and examined my hands. The two of them looked at me for a while.
I smiled and felt like an animal at the zoo, but I also had a
tremendous feeling of well-being. They began a negotiation
about whether I had a wooden spleen or a blocked liver. They
looked at me again and asked me to stick out my tongue again.
I felt myself giggling, glad to be part of this mystery to be
solved. Why couldn't I get pregnant?

In the end, we settled on Ren 6, 4, 2; some chi-building
and smoothing out of my liver. Whatever that meant. I closed
my eyes when they got out the needles and didn't open them
again until they had adjusted the heat lamps over me and shut
the door. I could hear the rain on the window in the little
room. "Twenty minutes," Dr. Ye said.

I could feel the needles only in this weird pulling of energy. Strings of energy. It felt great just to rest, sprawled out
on the table, breathing. As I meditated, I could feel the old
pain from my foot, from my bike accident. I had never gone to
the doctor after my accident—no money or insurance—but
I'm sure I had broken my foot. Now I was finally letting that
go. The mistakes that couldn't be righted, the regret for
what was but will never be again. Inevitably things go astray,
roads are taken that lead nowhere. But now I was on a new

path. I had never done anything like this—nurturing myself—before. It felt wildly luxurious, and it felt right.

While I turned to needles, Bill told me he would be driving to Arizona.

"What for?" I asked.

"To return the skull."

"What skull?"

"The one we took from the Indian land." He pointed at a cow skull that I had hung on our living room wall. I had never properly cleaned it, so it was always dropping a film of dust and it smelled weird. But it did look cool, like some Georgia O'Keeffe painting.

"Huh?" I said. "We found that on the ground." It was a find from the road trip we took after leaving Seattle for good.

"Native ground," he said. He was worried the theft had jinxed us. That it hadn't been a scrotal temperature problem this whole time, but one of bad juju. He went on to say he had been reading a book, *Coyote Medicine: Lessons from Native American Healing*, that suggested that unknown psychic spirits can affect your life.

I raised an eyebrow. Bill's usually so pragmatic; this sounded like a bunch of woo-woo BS. "Billy," I said. "You sound like my dad. Crazy."

He shrugged. But then again, I was having needles inserted into my body in a bid to get stronger baby-making chi. So who's more crazy?

A week later he and his friend Julie drove to Arizona and deposited the skull to its rightful place on the reservation. They also did mushrooms at Big Sur.

During his absence, I had cooked up my bag of Chinese fertility-enhancing herbs. Roots and berries that I slow cooked in water for twelve hours in a ceramic crock, which gave off an acrid stench and turned the water black. Once it cooled, I took a dose: it tasted like burned coffee with sour berry; the aftertaste was pure dirt.

Bill got back, mission accomplished. He said, in his mushroom haze that left him giggly and with a perma-smile, that the trees were the answer. They knew so much. I just nodded my head. I looked at the empty wall where the skull had hung, and I swear, I felt a renewed sense of hope and energy. I sipped some more of my herb brew. There had been a time in our lives when Bill and I had actively made fun of crystal-charging nut balls. But now, here we were: nut balls.

In March I still wasn't pregnant. My goat Bebe had kidded in October and was in heat again. That's how long it was taking me to get pregnant. I was getting lapped by a goat.

One day she escaped. I heard her calls near the front of the house and went running downstairs to find her in the street. I called her name, I pleaded, but I couldn't catch her. Then she headed toward Martin Luther King Jr. Way. She seemed to have a plan, her eyes were so focused, and she was letting out small cries while her hooved feet clattered on the pavement. When she reached the busy intersection, without looking, she began to cross the street, just as a bright orange lowrider displaying twenty-two-inch wheels passed by. Their encounter played out in slow-mo for me: my goat's spotted body out in the middle of the street; the driver, with his windows down, stereo up. He didn't have time to even look surprised, he just used one cool hand to glide the car out of the goat's path.

Safely across the street, Bebe looked kind of bored, like a teenager at an all-ages show. Suddenly, a punk girl dressed in black emerged out of nowhere and collared Bebe. The girl waited for me to run up, breathless, to reclaim my errant, horny goat. I noticed the girl was wearing a tattered sweatshirt with a patch that read "Courage" in death metal script.

"Thank you," I said. "Thank you, thank you! She's in heat," I explained. The girl scowled. Damn breeders.

To remedy the escaping horny goat problem, I brought home a stud goat named Mr. Lincoln from a farm up in Vacaville. He sat up front with me in my truck on the way to my house.

Mr. Lincoln enjoyed our farm. Plenty of good alfalfa, clean water, slightly cooler temperatures than Vacaville, which got infernally hot, even in March. As for the girls, they were avoiding him. Even though Bebe had been horny enough to escape, she suddenly didn't seem interested. She and her daughter climbed up onto the back stairs while Lincoln waited at the bottom, lips curled out, trying to catch a whiff of them. He couldn't climb very far up the stairs before he got scared and let out little cries until I came out of the house and rescued him. Mostly he seemed interested in eating.

Lincoln slept outside, under the stars, alone in a nest of discarded hay and sawdust because the does wouldn't even let him bed down with them. *He better get busy*, I thought when I surveyed the dwindling hay barn (a "shed" made by setting up two pallets on end and placing a heavy piece of wood on top of them).

One day I rounded the corner to the backyard and saw only Mr. Lincoln's back legs, moving forward and backward, forward and backward. Was he having sex? Finally! But as I got closer, I saw that no, he had just found the perfect spot to rub his neck—on my bike pedal. He looked like he was in a trance, just rubbing and rubbing; he didn't even look up at me when I stood over him. Meanwhile, the does sat up on the back porch, watching in disgust.

Bill took to making fun of Mr. L. He started talking in a quivering old man's voice, pretending to be the goat: "Let's see here, first I gotta get something to eat, and then I might just take a nap . . ." And though I laughed at Bill's Mr. Lincoln impersonation, I will admit that I had started to look at Bill in the same light.

At my regular acupuncture appointment, I told the people needling me—two young Chinese guys—that I was feeling really stressed out. They grew silent. Then finally one of them said, in halting English: "Does your boyfriend beat you?" I don't know if it was the way he said it, or me imagining the preposterous image of Bill hitting me, but I started laughing really hard. "No," I said, tears rolling down my face, "he doesn't beat me." He maybe couldn't get me pregnant, and I was slowly starting to accept that as a possibility. I started coming up with Plans B and C—perhaps we would go on a year-long bicycling trip; maybe we would move to Mexico. I came to see my future as plastic, flexible.

After a few weeks of hosting Mr. Lincoln with no action, I came upon a disturbing scene in the backyard. I smelled it first. Then I heard the yelling.

The does were making a high-pitched cry I had never heard before. Mr. Lincoln's penis was out—pink and long, and it was somehow spraying urine out in a fine mist, not a steady stream, but in a fan-shape, like the mister setting on a garden hose.

Then he was up, riding the doe though she was much taller than him. His lips were curled up in a grimace. Both of them were making a strange calling noise—it stuttered and crested and sounded strangely like hearing someone talking excitedly behind a heavy door. Mr. Lincoln's tongue was similar to Kiss guitarist Gene Simmons's, and he was utilizing it in a similar, showman kind of way. This went on for two days in my backyard. Friends would come over for a visit, peek in at the goats, would say, "whoa," and slowly back away. A real goat fuck.

How did I know the deed was done? The girls seemed really satisfied. Geriatric Mr. L got invited to sleep with them at night. And then I took him back to Vacaville. He sat up front with me like a pet dog in my farm truck—a rusty 1981 Datsun. I ate an orange and threw the peel on the floor of the truck. This truck, and its disarray of garbage and farm implements, mirrored my dad's messy Ford.

Instead of trying to purge this behavior, I'd kind of embraced it. It dawned on me that yes, I'm the kind of person who throws the orange peels on the floor and plans to pick them up but never does, who drives thrashed cars with dome lights that don't work, and will never work. I tend to be graceless, free-falling through life without saying excuse me.

While I was thinking this deep thought, I suddenly smelled goat poo. Mr. L had laid some hot goat berries directly where I buckled my seat belt. At Vacaville, Mr. L's home farm, Lincoln clattered out of the truck, and I flicked the goat turds out of the seat without much concern.

Just as the goats got knocked up, I finally did too.

I knew I was pregnant when, one day, the goat milk tasted

funny. It had a barnyard flavor to it, like it had gone bad. But the milk was fresh and new. Just yesterday it had tasted fabulously creamy. I put the glass down. Later in the day, my stomach felt strange, like it was stretching and churning. I went to Rite Aid to buy a pregnancy test.

The line at the downtown pharmacy was always slow and long. I stood there, pregnancy test in hand.

"Hey, Novella," Mac called. Mac was one of our queer friends who wanted to be called *zhe*, not she or he.

"Oh, hey," I said. I crossed my arms and tucked the EPT test away from sight.

"We're having another cabaret," Mac said. Bill and I loved going to these, Mac was a great host, and the acts were always weird and fun.

"Terrific," I nodded. *Oh god, don't let zher notice the pregnancy test.* We hadn't told many people that we were trying to conceive. Mac, I was pretty sure, wouldn't approve of this breeding thing Bill and I were up to. I felt like a sell-out, like a pirate turned merchant marine, Thunderbird-sipper turned wine snob, a hipster urban farmer turned stroller-pushing mommy.

Finally, it was my turn, and Mac flitted off, and I rushed home with the ultimate breeder purchase. In the safety of my bathroom I tore open the pregnancy test and peed onto the little stick. I watched with pure fascination as capillary action drew my urine across the marker that could sense the pregnancy hormones in my urine. First it was negative, a solid blue stripe that I had seen many times before. I let out my breath, pulled my pants up. Looked in the mirror.

I was really starting to look like my mother. She had just come to visit last month, to put the pressure on the whole getting knocked up thing. She had rented a car, and one night drove up to Berkeley to look for her old house. "I don't know what I'm looking for," she said, embarrassed. But I understood that desire to go back in time.

In the mirror I saw that I had bags under my eyes, and my crow's-feet fanned down across my cheeks. When my mom was thirty-eight, she had already had two kids, raised us from babies to toddlers to kids. We had gone to kindergarten, she had divorced my dad, gotten a job, moved to Washington State. I, in contrast, was just starting this process.

Then I looked down at the pregnancy test, flush with urine, and saw a plus sign had formed.

That afternoon Bill came home early. I was out in the garden, trying to catch an escaped rabbit who disappeared behind the back of the chicken coop.

"Help me, Monk," I said.

He went to one end of the coop and waved a branch at the rabbit. I waited at the other end. She scooched toward the safe middle, and I squeezed behind the coop until I could grab her. She made little grunting noises, and I realized that she was pregnant too—that's why she was looking for a hiding spot. I found a nesting box for the bunny, stuffed it with straw, and put her in the cage with it. After closing the door to the cage, I looked up at Bill and blurted out, "I'm pregnant."

Bill puffed up like a rooster. "I did it!" he crowed.

Riana and Novella riding stick horses on the ranch, 1976.

Twelve

When I was five months pregnant, I flew to France.

My sister met me at the airport. Though we talk on the phone weekly, the high price of flights meant I hadn't seen her since right after she had given birth to Amaya, five years ago. Her time spent raising her daughter had been good to her—she looked fit and happy. In addition to growing most of their family's food, she collected lots of wild stuff too. Amaya was growing up on the land, running free like we had on the ranch. There was now even a name for it—free-range parenting—and my sister had embraced the philosophy.

I waddled toward Riana, trashed from the long flight. She looked glowing, vibrant, full of life, dressed in tight jeans and a pair of high boots. When she hugged me, she felt lithe and strong. I felt squishy, like ripe fruit. I had been eating like a horse, sometimes waking up in the middle of the night to graze on nuts and ice cream. I was looking forward to being in France and eating as much cheese, bread, and charcuterie as possible.

Instead of buying food, though, we ended up mostly foraging, the way we had as kids. We went clam digging and elderberry collecting, harvested figs from trees growing in the village. We even went to a pond where we collected cattails to cook and gave ourselves mud baths.

"There are all these feral vineyards," Riana said on one of my last days there. "The grapes are so good!" She got a look in her eye that promised I wouldn't be disappointed. So we packed the car with baskets, pulled out of the stone gate that surrounded their house, and drove into the countryside. The Opel bumped along, passing field after field of grapes. Their dog, Zach, stuck his nose out the window, all aquiver. It was September and the *vendage* was on, so workers were in every field, picking grapes by hand, placing them in lug trays, which were then poured into enormous hoppers loaded onto the back of tractors. It was a timeless process—in fact, this was the same way grapes were harvested when my parents were in France picking grapes so many years ago.

Benji turned off the paved road and we set across a bumpy dirt track that ran into the fields of grapes. He's got dark hair and eyes, and when his DNA met my sister's, these dominant traits were passed onto Amaya. She was gorgeous, with long dark hair and olive skin. She sat in the back with me, eyeing my bulging stomach.

"There's a sour cherry tree there," Riana said, and pointed toward a riverbank where lots of different trees were jumbled together. I saw it, some dried fruit still clinging to the branches.

"Nobody picks this stuff?" I asked.

"No!" Benji and Riana both yelled, as if they couldn't believe it themselves. "It's crazy, Novella," Riana said, turning to look at me in the backseat with Amaya.

Suddenly, we were there. There were signs that the field had once been in production, but the wooden support beams had rotted and crumbled so the grapes had resorted to scrambling across the ground. They were not trained against the metal wire like the grapes we had seen from the road.

"Taste one!" Riana urged.

Never one to stick a toe in, I grabbed an entire cluster and stuffed it into my mouth. I was actually really hungry. A hundred sweet explosions in my mouth went off as I chewed on the grapes. A hint of tart, but only a little. They were warm from the summer sun, and the skins were just slightly chewy. I grabbed the next closest cluster and ate more. I looked down at Amaya and she was doing the same thing.

We got out our baskets and began collecting. Walking along the fallen fence, pausing to clip the heavy fruit. The air was so clean, so crisp. The soil was chocolate brown. The leaves had just started to blush red, and the rolling hills of vines were stunning. Walking along next to my sister, I was reminded of the ranch. I also thought of my parents—not far from here they had been picking grapes together, planning a family.

A little while later, Riana and I sat in the car, waiting for Benji to take Amaya for a potty under a tree.

"God, she's all grown up," I said. I was surprised at how having a child had changed my sister. Right after giving birth to Amaya, my sister began living a more ecological lifestyle. She didn't want to use disposable diapers, and so made her own diaper inserts and wipes. As Amaya got older, her fervor to save the earth grew stronger: she and Benji stopped using toilet paper; they stopped buying stuff and started dumpster diving and foraging. Some more Dad traits surfaced: Riana learned how to use a chainsaw and started channeling her psychic abilities. She had gotten into exploring her past lives and studying the moon cycles.

We watched Amaya pull up her pants, skipping along

back to the car, pausing to pick up a stick. Amaya was so perfect, so beautiful.

"You know, she saved me," said Riana.

"Who?"

"Amaya."

"What do you mean?" I asked. I think I knew but I wanted her to explain.

After a pause, she told me something I had never heard. That she had struggled with mental illness. Suicidal tendencies.

"I thought about killing myself, even when I was pregnant with Amaya."

I gasped, clutched my stomach. "No."

"Yes. But then, after I had her, Novella, something in me changed. It cracked open, and the love came pouring in. She saved me. She made me."

I grabbed her hand and we were quiet for a while, feeling all the past swirling around us.

Before I left for France, I had sent Dad an e-mail message telling him my news. He wrote back his congratulations, told me that I would be a great mom, just like Pat. Terribly wonderful, I thought, remembering his haiku.

"I wish we could have saved Dad," I said.

"Don't you think we did?" she asked. Then Benji and Amaya were back and we drove home. Maybe we did.

That night, lying in the guest bedroom upstairs, I was awoken by their little town's church bells, which rang on the hour. The baby liked to move around at night, and busily kicked my ribs. I pulled down the covers and watched the alien movements across my stomach.

We were going to have a girl. Just before leaving for

France, I had an ultrasound appointment. The technician lubed up an ultrasound wand and stuck it against my swollen stomach. We were looking for internal organs and body parts. The heart, the kidneys. The baby bobbed around, and I loved the chance to see her instead of just feeling her nudges in my womb. The technician pointed out her brain, her lips, her stomach. We had a tough time finding the baby's feet, and the technician wildly prodded my stomach with the ultrasound wand. I started to worry. I could feel the baby swimming around low, down near my cervix, which tickled. Then finally the fetus flipped around and we saw her foot—it was tiny, and looked like a badger's paw. Then the other one. I was relieved. She would be able to walk. Then we looked for her hands. I had bargained with myself: If she were missing arms or hands, that would be OK. They make all these great bionic arms. . . . But then the technician found them—two perfect hands. One was making the Ozzy sign. The bones in her arms glowed white, and I could see each individual digit. That's when I started crying. Despite our obvious genetic flaws, Bill and I had put together a healthy baby.

As I lay there in the dark French countryside, I thought of my parents, who had been here before, conceiving Riana. They had been young and hopeful, idealistic and enchanted with each other. Those days must still hold some magic for them. I know they do for me—I grew up listening to my mom's stories about their great adventures.

My sister once told me that I always try to find the answers. Instead she tries to find the beginning of everything. I remember being annoyed and not fully understanding what she meant. It's true that I do always look for an answer, something to explain why things are the way they are. Now I was here, where my parents had lived out the happiest part of their relationship. I realized that their beginning was just as important, as real, as their ending. There had been a moment of great love for them. To return to their stomping grounds felt like I had made it back to the beginning.

A few days later I flew home. "Have a great labor!" Riana joked. I waved. "Oh, yeah," I said, "I've been watching the goats!" And I winked.

Eight months into my pregnancy, a burst of progesterone coursed through my body. The hormone gave my hair lushness and bounce. My skin cleared up for the first time since third grade. Men regularly stopped me in the street, asking for my phone number, even though I was clearly knocked up. My dream state had changed too. Instead of my usual anxiety dreams about failing a test or missing a train, I experienced pleasant, almost psychedelic dreams. One that stuck with me featured a group of Civil War veterans on horseback. They wore big beards—and, in the dream, I loved them, felt tender and grateful to them. I also once dreamed of my father as a boy—we were playing a game: I would make a scary face and then he would make the same face. In the dream, at first I was scared of his bulging eyes, but then I realized it was just a game, and started laughing.

Bill and I, embracing our inner nut ball, enrolled in a mindful childbirth class, though we had a hard time taking it seriously. "I just had a mindful poop," Bill would say, flushing the toilet. "Can you mindfully wash the dishes?" I would say, snickering. But one night, that class busted me wide open.

We were doing an exercise where we looked into each other's eyes and repeated some things the teacher, a crone-like midwife, said. There I was, belly huge, on a bouncy ball chair, staring into Bill's eyes. "I am ready to have a child with you," all the couples said in unison, looking into each other's eyes, "and this child will hold us together for as long as we are alive." As we said the words to each other, suddenly the enormity of the thing hit us. Bill and I both teared up. Though we weren't going to get married, having a child would be as close to marriage as we would come.

Like my parents, when I was pregnant Billy and I bought some land together. Not 180 acres, but one-tenth of an acre, the empty lot next to our apartment that we had been squatting on for going on eight years. The owner of the land tracked us down and offered to sell it to us. The recession had lingered and they couldn't get funding to build condos like they had once hoped. The price was right: $30,000, the same amount my parents had forked over in 1971 for their ranch.

Bill and I cashed in all our savings to buy it. After the paperwork had been processed, I wandered out to the lot and walked all forty-five hundred square feet of it with a new sense of ownership. Being a squatter, there had been no real plan. Willy-nilly I had planted vegetables and fruit trees, with no eye toward the future. Maybe I didn't want to get attached. I was just surviving on a short-term basis, knowing one day I would be pushed off the land.

As I walked and observed, I had regrets about things I had done when I had been a squatter, like planting a plum tree too close to an apple tree or letting the Bermuda grass take over. Now was my chance to dig in, the place was truly mine.

My plan was to clear out my old mistakes and build anew. I actually hired someone to build a functional chicken coop, where I could raise my chickens and ducks. I attacked the Bermuda grass, channeling my energy toward this task.

I also got a hold of some historical maps of the area and

discovered that before the lot had been vacant, it had been an apartment building with a small grocery store on the ground floor. They sold meat and vegetables at this store. Now I grew meat and vegetables in the footprint of the building. Rhyming, not repeating.

Preparations for the baby began to take over. Bill spent an entire afternoon wrestling with an umbrella stroller someone had handed down to us, trying to open it. There were so many baby items that required special knowledge and skill. I knew how to milk a goat and slaughter a chicken, but installing—and adjusting—a baby car seat? Folding up a stroller? Impossible. Bill's a handy guy, up for the challenge, so I let him fiddle with the thing. I never planned on using it—I was going to wear my baby like an indigenous woman from a third world country. But Bill has a bad back. When someone offered us a stroller, we took it.

"What do you think of the name Babette?" I asked Bill. I'd just spent an hour writing out names for our daughter on a piece of paper like a lovesick eighth grader. "I like Louise too," I said. Bill made a face. Bill's mom had weighed in: She liked Sarah, but this didn't seem right. My mom was so excited she couldn't hardly believe it. Literally. She would send me e-mails asking, "Are you still pregnant?"

I had been thinking about her former self, sitting in the A-frame in Crescent, feverishly knitting baby clothes and reading Dr. Spock. At night, when the baby was moving around the most, Bill would bend over my pregnant belly, listening to the baby move around, smoothing my belly with his gentle, callused hands. I couldn't help but think of my dad. Maybe he did the same thing.

Suddenly Bill figured out the secret, and the stroller folded out with a satisfying popping noise. He showed me the hidden lever to pull. I bought eco-paint and painted the baby room a pale green color. I hung a mobile over the changing table. I collected cloth diapers and learned how they worked. I was nesting like the rabbits out on my front deck.

However, as much as I was nesting like a bunny, my rabbits were starting to disgust me. It must have been hormones, but I had grown to loathe them. I could barely bring myself out to the deck to feed them. It wasn't their smell—which can be quite fragrant—it was their demeanor. Timid and meek, hiding in their nesting boxes. It used to be so cute when they humped furiously, tails pumping. But now, watching the act made me hate them. I touched my bloated stomach and felt repulsed. Maybe I had become a self-loathing breeder, but they had to go.

I put out an ad on an urban homestead listserv, and within one day the rabbits and their cages were cleared out. My mouth tightened as I watched the rabbits disappear.

I had my front deck back. I maniacally scrubbed away years of splattered rabbit pee off the walls, power washed the floor, and put down a fresh coat of paint. Then I went to a hardware store and bought a gas BBQ to put on the deck. Even as I lit my new grill and roasted some ears of corn with a sense of satisfaction, I knew I was creeping toward what I have avoided my whole life: ease, comfort. The rabbit cleanse made me wonder how exactly I was going to raise a farm and a kid.

As the months marched on and my belly expanded, I felt more and more exhausted. Even though I owned it, the garden went fallow, then feral. I could only focus on one thing, even though at that point it was out of my control: making the baby.

Novella and Mom in the vegetable
garden on the ranch, 1975.

Novella and Frannie on the
urban farm, 2012.

Thirteen

This is punishment, I thought, panting. I was perched on a hospital bed, legs splayed out. I had just taken another shit on the hospital bed. I had been so cavalier about birth. That wink. In the back of my mind, I knew it was going to be painful. But not this painful.

I had walked to the hospital. Not because I'm a badass, but because I couldn't bear the thought of getting into a car while having a contraction. So I walked with my doula while Bill followed along with us, slowly, in the car. It was a remarkably clear and bright December morning. Our neighborhood of Ghost Town was just starting to wake up. A few shopping-cart guys were cruising around. Every few minutes I would stop walking, lean up against a building, and have a contraction, groaning in pain.

The contractions had started in the late evening, so painful I couldn't even see clearly. Later I learned I was having back labor from the baby's head moving against my pelvis.

The pain mounted and mounted until I had blinders on, and could only see a few inches in front of me. My eyes were unfocused, my pupils enormous.

Someone whisked my poo away, and I felt grateful for half a second. I tried to breathe as I got ready for the next painful wave of contractions in my uterus. My uterus was actively trying to churn the baby out. What's amazing is the little baby, not even born, knows how to wiggle and turn down the birth canal to get herself out.

Why it had to be so painful seemed wrong. I was trying to observe the pain of childbirth, like I had learned in our mindfulness class. I wanted to listen to it, and find it fascinating. But I discovered that actually pain made me want to run.

Everyone disappeared for a while. I had the vague sense that Bill was updating his Facebook status with new birth developments when I wasn't having a contraction. When I was having a contraction, and had to push, Bill and the doula would each grab one leg and pin it behind my head. I had this idea that I would be on all fours, like a goat, and the baby would just slide out. Wrong. I would grunt and pant—and poop—while a full minute of absolute agony ripped through my body. After each push a nurse would tell me the baby had progressed a couple centimeters down the birth canal.

"How long is this going to take?" I had my eye on the clock, and vaguely sensed that I had been in active pushing labor for over five hours. I had been in labor—having painful contractions every five minutes or so—for almost twenty-four hours. My mom had labored to have Riana for only eight hours, and me for only six hours. Imagining birthing times might be hereditary, I had been betting on an easy labor, and now I was losing. A strange thought crossed my mind—I was giving birth like my father would have given birth. Fighting, cussing, scared. I was feeling wronged, like the universe had conspired against me. Trapped and feral. I needed help.

The staff wheeled a full-length mirror in front of me. I strained to see what was going on. Things down there sure looked messed up. Somehow the backs of my legs looked bruised. I really should have shaved. In good news, my vagina looked like a lotus.

I peered at the mirror. I couldn't see much. My eyes had gotten really puffy from the effort of pushing. So much for the joyous photos of mom and babe, where mom looks radiant like the Virgin Mary. I could see a head.

A wave of pain arrived. I started howling. Deep groaning guttural howls. I arched my head up like I remember the goat doing, stretching, stretching. Then I realized that this was it. I had to die. I had to make the jump, to do the thing that I had resisted for so long. I bared down, became pure animal, not human. I went someplace else. They say the ring of fire—when the baby's head passes out the vagina—is the most painful part, but I don't remember that. I just remember hearing a keening wail, and the feeling that I had just taken the biggest dump of my life, and then Frannie was born.

She was bigger than I thought she would be, and she smelled sweet and milky. The nurses put her on my belly, and she slithered up, on her own, toward my breast. Babies' instincts are strong. They know where the breast is and will crawl toward it because of a special scent the breast emits. But also because babies can see the nipple. In the last weeks of my pregnancy, my nipples and areola had turned dark brown. This contrast served as a signpost for baby: MILK HERE.

She looked just like Bill's dad—with a square old-man

face and a thatch of red hair. Bill took photos of the event, and it took me weeks before I could finally look at them, to see what had happened to me, what I had done.

Bill dialed my mom on his phone and held her up to my ear.

"I can't believe you did this," I shouted.

"Yup. It's a big thing," Mom said. She was suddenly my new hero.

Some women fall in love with their babies at first sight. I didn't fall completely in love with baby Frannie until the second night we were together. We brought her home from the hospital, bundled up and red-faced. She woke me up that night, around three a.m., after sleeping for quite a few hours. She seemed to have a smile on her face, like she wanted to tell me something, some secret. Maybe it was gas, but that smile destroyed the old me, and in its place someone else emerged. This was forever, in a way nothing had been before.

Friends had milked my goats while I lay in bed recovering from the birth for the first two weeks. On Christmas, six days after she was born, I limped down the backstairs with Frannie. I introduced her to the goats. They were curious and excited to smell the newborn baby. I snapped photos of Frannie in the goat manger, surrounded by her new caprine friends.

A few weeks later, I was finally strong enough to start milking the goats. I opened up the back door and called out to Bebe. "Come on up!" I shouted. She clattered up the stairs and jumped onto the milk stand. I sat behind her, like I had done hundreds of times, washed off her udder with a wipe, and began milking.

It was back to the old routine, this time with Frannie snuggled up next to me in a sling. For the first minutes of milking, she quietly slept. Then, maybe smelling the goat, or the goat milk that was steadily being drawn into the bucket, Frannie started to wail. It was a newborn's mewling sound, and it made Bebe nervous. She started to shift her legs about, and even raised up her back leg to kick me. I caught her leg in one hand, held the milk pail in the other. *Jesus, I need a hubcap*, I thought, *like my mom had used.* Then I noticed that Bebe wasn't the only one letting down her milk. My breasts, hearing the sound of my baby, started oozing out breast milk.

That's when I knew the goats weren't going to last. There could only be one lactating animal on my farm, and that was me. And it wasn't just the milking: it was the challenge of cleaning out the goat pens, trimming their hooves, or throwing bales of alfalfa around—all while carrying around a little baby.

Instead of taxing myself to the limit like my parents had, I let it slip. Unlike my mom, who had depended on the farm for her survival, I had the choice.

The goat diaspora began. A prize doeling named Gretel went to a friend in East Oakland. Milky Way went to a delightful gay hairdresser from Hollister. Bebe went to live in a farm near Sacramento. While I watched Bebe get loaded up and disappear, I thought how I had once thought of the goats like my children. They taught me about how to care for them, how to love. My goats had been like those stuffed animals I used to bring to elementary school. They made the world feel safe; they showed me how to be human.

Six weeks after the birth, Bill and I were like zombies. Frannie wouldn't sleep through the night. We had taken to going on long walks with her in a sling at odd hours, hoping that might lull her back into a deep slumber. One night, walking out on the main drag near our house near two in the morning, we passed by a bus stop. A man with a shopping cart was stretched out on the bench there. We scurried by him, me carrying baby Frannie in a sling. He called out to us. "Hey," he said. We shuffled along faster, ignoring him, thinking he was going to ask for spare change. "You got get that baby on a schedule!" he admonished. "How?" I said, stopping in my tracks. For several minutes, the man went on a point-by-point description of how to better accommodate the child's napping needs during the day, and advised us to let her cry it out at night. We nodded, grateful for any advice, even from the homeless.

The next morning, I was nursing the baby and talking to Bill when I noticed he looked like he was about to cry.

"What is it, babe?" I asked him. Frannie had fallen asleep, a trickle of milk drooled out of the corner of her mouth. She was tiny, still larval, snuggled into a swaddling blanket.

"Do you love Frannie more than me?" he said after a moment.

"Yes," I said, without hesitation.

"Good, because that's how I feel too," Bill said. Bill looked exhausted but glowing. I felt the same. Tired, but happy to change her dirty diapers, which always held a strange green goo. Must have been the hormones, which must have soaked into Bill's bloodstream too. We smiled at each other.

After I sent Dad word of Frannie's arrival, and a photo of her in the goat manger, Dad had sent me a gift. It was a transistor radio, carefully wrapped in a blanket that reeked of wood smoke. There was no note. I called him to share how parenthood was going. He was surprisingly lucid. I asked him what I had been like as a baby. "You were so carefree and easygoing," he said, and I heard him sniffing. "The love of my life."

If Dad could be so swept away by a zucchini blossom, my mind reeled at how he must have reacted to a baby. He must have loved our translucent eye lids. The rosebud lips. The strange, gray eyes of a newborn. The fingers, so perfect. I thought, for the first time, about how hard it must have been for him when we left. The memory of holding us in his arms, which were now empty, must have been a torture. But maybe those remembrances of us kept him alive, like my sister had said. That we had saved him, maybe even carried him through those times when he was barely holding on.

Grandpa George and Frannie, 2013.

Fourteen

When Frannie was almost a year and a half, Riana and I took her to Orofino to meet her grandpa. We bought the airline tickets to Idaho on a whim when Riana came for a visit. I hadn't been back since the time I had broken into my dad's cabin, three years before.

Instead of telling Dad we would be in town—remembering that he might flee if we told him we were coming—we dropped in for a sneak visit. Orofino had spiffed up in the three years since I had last been there. New businesses had sprung up and a scruffiness had vanished. Riana and I had a plan to track Dad down. We knew his pattern: a few games of pool in the morning, then the library. We figured we would cruise Main Street, pull over when we saw him, and introduce him to his newest granddaughter.

Unfortunately, there happened to be a logger conference in town that weekend. Every hotel was booked. The sidewalks were filled with men who looked just like our dad. We drove around in our rented Prius. "Is that him?" I said, slowing down to point at a craggy old guy wearing a Stihl hat.

"No, no. Too tall," Riana said. When trying to pick Dad out from the throng of loggers, all of them wearing flannels and dirty Levi's, didn't work, we resorted to e-mailing him from the library. We sent him word that we were in town and he should meet us at the park. Then we went there and waited.

That morning we had gone back up to the land. The thimbleberry bushes hadn't leafed out yet but the huckleberries had. Waterfalls tumbled off of sheer rock and wildflowers popped out of every crevice. We had passed Max's house, and I noticed that he hadn't planted those peach trees after all.

"Stop the car!" my sister yelled. I slammed on the brakes. "What?" I said.

"I feel something," she said. I rolled my eyes. I looked around. Just forest, the same forest we had been driving through for miles. She got out of the car, left the door open. A plastic bottle filled with river water that she had insisted we collect for our trip up to the ranch sloshed on the dash.

The car shut off. I checked on Frannie, who was blissfully asleep, in a car seat in the back. So much had changed in my life since her birth. I had become an absolute baby lover, stopping mothers in the street so I could hold their little ones, noting their plump little wrists and diving in to smell their heads. Bill changed too. One day, holding Frannie, he said: "I love the smell of diapers!" and grinned at how idiotic that was.

I watched Riana jump over a barbed-wire fence. She was

still thin and healthy looking. She was wearing a pair of suede boots and tight lowrider jeans. She tiptoed across the forest into a glade.

Even though she was otherwise healthy, she had been having strange episodes of vertigo every few months. The French doctors assured her it wasn't MS—which we are both scared we'll inherit from Mom. When the vertigo hit, my sister would have visions. Visions of a Native American spirit guide. He told her she could cleanse the ranch of the evil. I laughed uneasily when she told me that story. How can a scientist explain such things, such premonitions? I just nodded, thinking of Satanic chipmunks and wondering if magical thinking might be hereditary too. While I was dubious of healing the ranch, I was curious to see the place again, and especially with my sister for the first time in twenty-three years.

From the driver's seat I scanned the forest, looking for Riana. There she was: holding her hand up to a big pine tree. Then she hugged the tree. "Frannie, your aunt is crazy," I muttered. She just snored away. Then I heard a shout and Riana ran toward me. She was clutching something in her hands. I got out of the car and met her in the middle of the road. She held up two enormous morel mushrooms.

"Oh my god," I said.

"The forest told me these were here," she said. I grabbed one of the mushrooms and took a deep breath of the fungi. Just as I remembered: meaty, oaky, forest.

"And I got a rose too." she held up a Woods' rose, *Rosa woodsii*, the wild rose that was in bloom when she was born, that I had picked rosehips from when Dad and I had our reunion near the ranch.

"OK," I said, "let's go." We drove until we got to the spot where our mom used to stop when the road got too rough and there was snow on the ground. I strapped Frannie into a front pack, Riana loaded up the bottle of Clearwater River water and the rose, and we hiked in.

We didn't talk much as we hiked uphill. It was warm and the gravel road crunched under our feet, the river water sloshed. A few of the wild apple trees that grew along the road looked dead, but the ponderosa pines looked fine, letting out a low whistle as the wind rippled through their branches.

Our early childhood had been so idyllic. I couldn't help compare it to how I was raising Frannie. In Oakland, she picked fruit from the trees, yanked up carrots. She dodged broken glass and danced a little jig when a lowrider with a thumping sound system cruised by. She couldn't run free like Riana and I had, but she was as feral as you can get while living in a city.

Having a kid made me think of time differently. I had planted an orchard of fruit trees: espaliered apples, peaches, and plums. I planted grape vines, long-term crops like asparagus, and a hedge of citrus trees. It would take about eight years for the fruit trees to start bearing a good crop. By then, I would be forty-seven years old, Bill would be fifty-one, and Frannie would be in fourth grade.

Becoming a property owner, I understood how my father must have felt when he lost the ranch—even though it was through his own failings. That emptiness, that hope dashed, all that potential, gone. What are you after you've lost everything you loved? I didn't want to ever imagine that. I clung to the people whom I loved—Bill, Frannie, my sister, my mom, my friends.

. . .

Riana and I crested the hill, where the trailer had been, and beyond, the old site of the Rough House. The last time I had come to the ranch, I didn't get to look around the property much. There had been that woman in the house and she seemed skeptical of me. I told Riana that this might happen, that people aren't necessarily open to strangers, even if the strangers grew up on this land. It wasn't ours anymore.

"The pond!" Riana said, pointing at the reedy water. Two ducks spooked and took flight.

No one was around. In fact, the whole property felt abandoned. A shed next to the new house was open and empty. There were no cars, just a parked RV. We scurried toward the spot where the Rough House had been. We could see a concrete slab where the foundation had been. It was still scorched black, because the new owners were using the site as a burn pile area.

Riana, channeling her spirit guide, disappeared into the woods over a hill. I worried about people appearing, perhaps carrying shotguns. Frannie woke up and I sat under a tree, nursed her. On the ground, the spiky leaves of wild iris were coming up. Beyond them was the apple orchard, where Riana and I had picked that bumper crop of morels with Dad. I took a deep breath. The land smelled exactly as I remembered. The warm sweet pine needle smell mixed with the pond water and hot granite rocks.

Frannie saw a red-winged blackbird, pointed. "Doh." She called every animal she saw "doh"— dog, cat, bird.

In the span of a year, I had watched her learn how to smile, crawl, laugh, ask for help, walk, babble, climb up and down stairs. All on her own accord. It was instinct, desires encoded into her DNA, that led her to do these things.

In the next few years, she would learn how to talk in complete sentences, to jump and skip, to share, to learn from the animals. These are all human impulses, and though it seems like a miracle, all that learning, it's natural. Watching her grow, I realized that as we all age, we are always learning and changing, and that there are stages in our development, even after we have reached adulthood.

Looking back on my struggle to find my father, I began to understand my quest as part of a bigger human drive. My journey was triggered by my desire to have children, but whether we reproduce or not, the need to understand where we come from is universal. It's just part of the human process, like learning to talk, or to jump. We have an instinct to tell the story of our past, to understand what came before, to try to make sense of it.

For me, the answers weren't clear cut, and there are still mysteries that will never be recovered. But having come full circle—becoming a parent myself—I had a new lens to look through. Being here, back on the ranch, I could better imagine what my parents had been up to. Their struggles and the challenges that children bring—but also the fun. I imagined myself visiting them, as a friend now. I don't feel that hot anger of youth, where everything is supposed to be ideal. People do their best, and that's what my parents were doing. I also am preparing myself for the day when Frannie will ask me these same questions. She might wonder why I chose such a wild life for her.

After a few minutes, Riana came back to the clearing where the house had been.

"I did it," she reported. "Planted the rose, gave it some

river water. Then I found this," she held up an enormous morel mushroom. This one was fresher than the other ones she found. It was a light mousey color, like it had fruited just that morning. Frannie leaned in to smell the mushroom. Then our work was done. We hiked back to the car, and drove back to civilization.

At the Orofino park, I pushed Fran on the swings while Riana went to look at a yard sale being held in the park. I talked to Bill on the phone, then when I looked up I saw an old man, wearing a pair of baggy jeans, and two layers of shirts even though it was hot outside. He was looking for something. Dad.

"George," I yelled. Then I grabbed Frannie and walked toward him. "George! Dad!!"

He turned around. He had grown out his moustache so it was long and white.

"Stay back," he said, and held out his hand. "I'm sick, don't come within three feet of me." I stopped. I didn't want Frannie to get sick. "This is your granddaughter," I said. She pointed at him with a chubby finger.

"Gorgeous," he said. And he looked like he was about to faint. As we stood there, three feet apart from each other, I realized that I was the last of the Carpenters. Riana had taken Benji's name. My daughter had Bill's last name. Dad and I were the last Carpenters standing.

"Those eyes are intense, whoa!" Dad hooted. Frannie was staring him down with her gold-brown eyes. She pointed at him again.

"Let me go find Riana," I said and went to get her. I found her at a booth at the rummage sale, talking to a woman about past lives and how the universe is inside each and every one of us.

"Dad's here," I said.

"I thought I sensed him," she said and went outside to reunite with him. She hadn't seen him in five years. We hadn't seen him together since the 1980s and punishment summer.

"Stay back, I'm just coming out of some god-awful siege for six days," he said again to her. But my sister just laughed at that. "I'm immune, Dad. I'm immune." And she hugged him and I saw tears spring to his eyes as he held her. As Dad hugged her, and I kept Frannie at a safe distance, it was like watching him hug me. I felt proud of my sister—and later, myself. For going back to the source of so much pain, a place of discomfort. She was brave in her willingness to throw herself into the center of the fire, heart open.

We all sat down at a picnic table and my sister caught Dad up on all her happenings. Instead of talking, I chased after Frannie, who was not one to sit still for long. I wandered in and out of their conversation. At one point I heard my dad talking about that Beelzebub that was on the ranch. "We came all the way from Oregon, only to meet Satan." Riana explained that she had cleared him away; that she had a spirit guide who told her what had happened. Dad was speechless. She matched his craziness and raised him two.

"Dad, I just wanted to tell you that you weren't in my life, but that's OK," Riana said. "That's why I turned out how I did, and I'm proud of who I am. You've given us a crazy genius, and I want to thank you."

"It's not what I wanted," Dad mumbled.

Then it was time to go back to Lewiston and catch our

plane. Dad ambled off to his truck. Riana and I crossed through the park together one last time. "We did it," I said, Frannie cradled on my hip. My sister and I hugged each other, the sun strobing through the trees. We were finally done searching, and could say good-bye to Dad, to Orofino, unsure when we would see either again.

Novella and Dad, the old ranch property in the background, 2010.

Epilogue

It has been over four years since my dad went missing. He told me in an e-mail recently that he's stopped chopping wood. It's too hard on my body, he explained. He's become less and less lucid—sending several e-mails sometimes with basically the same message, as if he didn't remember writing them. The e-mails say that he tries to leave Idaho because the winters get so cold but when he gets on the road, he has a mental breakdown, and has to abort the trip.

On the rare occasions when we talk on the phone, he often repeats himself over and over again. I worry he is getting Alzheimer's or dementia. That one day, he will go completely feral, unable to take care of himself. For now, I've taken to sending him money—enough to shack up somewhere in town for the duration of the winter. When Riana hasn't heard from Dad in a while, she starts to worry. Then she calls the library in Orofino. The librarians there are exceedingly kind, and are happy to give her the Dad report. Sending money, getting updates from afar, it's all we can do. I now recognize that it's all he could do for us too.

On the way back from Idaho, the last time we saw Dad, my sister and I stopped off to see Mom. After a meal of Hood Canal shrimp and smoked salmon, Mom put us to work. We helped weed her garden, which she has been improving for over thirty years. Her work shows: She has a small orchard and berry patch, in addition to perennial beds of uncommon lushness and color.

Mom is still in touch with the Farm Out crowd, and friends from her days teaching school at Hood Canal. She has thrived, despite adversity, because of these friendships.

After garden chores, Riana and I scraped off the moss from the shingled roof. Then went up to the attic to clear it out. I was a hopeless hoarder and had stored stuff up there since I had left for college, and even after. Now I was forty years old, and it was time to finally purge the past.

Up in the attic, Riana and I laughed at our high school yearbooks and old notes from friends. Then I found a shoebox full of letters, mostly from Dad. Most of them dated from the 1990s, when I was in college. They are postmarked from Idaho, a few from his time in Alaska when he was working for the forest service there. As I read the old letters, they seem foreign and strange. They begin, "Hello Pumpkin," and sign off, "I love you totally." I don't remember getting them, and they reference events I don't remember. In one he described his bulldozer breaking down, another of pitching a tent on the ranch land and getting snowed on, another where he broke his arm. They are apologetic but proud, explaining that he had been a marginal dad but that I should give him space to be human and make mistakes. They are really the last thing I have from him, artifacts from a time when he was struggling, but still together.

As I read his letters to me, I could finally admit that I was partially to blame for our broken relationship. For my whole life, I had been shaped not by his presence, but by my imagined version of him. There was a time when I could have made him real, sought him out. But to do that I would have had to destroy my own creation. He was more palatable as a mythical creature. And, I suppose, he created me, imagined me as well. I could be perfect in his mind.

The final letter I found was a card with a painting of wolves, a quote from John Muir inside: "In God's wildness lies the hope of the world—the great fresh, unblighted, unredeemed wilderness." The letter begins with "Dear Daughter," and tells me he is glad that I read *Pan*. That it's a book you can go back to every few years and see in a different light. Then, I'm surprised to read, he writes: "One disclaimer: I'm not Glahn but I value many of the things he does—forest smells, the innocence of the animals, the hoarfrost on a severe winter landscape, the smell of spring . . ."

Families are like ecosystems. They begin looking one way, but as the years tick by, the inhabitants change. Some grow and flourish, others are wounded. They might rebound, or die. Nests are built and young are raised, then the fledglings leave. When disaster hits, only the adaptable survive. In my family, there were constants that added a certain texture to our family's ecosystem: love of language, of reading. A tendency toward living on the fringes. A hot rage that burns inside of us, and sometimes threatens ourselves and others. Sensitivity, a sense of the incredible power and beauty in the natural world. A love of the numinous so powerful that it mesmerizes us and inspires us. We are craggy and hard; intense and uncompromising.

More and more I see my father when I see photos of myself. My lips, when they snarl, a certain look in my eye that I can only see as coming directly from Dad. If I hadn't sought him out, these traits might be a mystery, like looking at a stranger. These days, I find the similarities between me and Dad vaguely comforting. I realize that every gesture that I do—how I put on a pair of socks, run my fingers through my hair, turn pages in a book—is a reflection of the people who created me. Every movement, every act, is a meditation on those who came before us.

As for Frannie, her personality comes out more and more each day. She has definitely inherited one thing from her granddad: a hooting laugh. When she first did the laugh, crinkling her nose just like he does, I recognized it as Dad's and fell in love with her some more. The life we have created for her might be hard, I understand that, and maybe one day she will rage against me, asking why. But I think she is ready for anything, as long as she knows we will always love her.

All these years I had thought Dad had been faking—like I had been—real love. But now that I have a child myself, I understand the all-consuming love that a child gives you. I could never love him like he loves me. I'm grateful that at least I had time with him, as painful as it was. I'm proud that I walked with the wild man that is my father, and I finally came to see him as human.

Acknowledgments

Though people like to describe the book writing process as a birth, I came to see this project more like timber clearing. Choosing which trees stay, which ones go—it wasn't easy, and I had to depend on others for perspective. The tenacious Lindsay Whalen, my editor and forewoman at Penguin, did just that, in addition to always keeping me on task when I flailed. My agent, Richard Morris, even fired up a chainsaw a couple of times. Phil Druker, builder of cabins and hiker of mountains, literally housed me in his past, shared stories, and even gave editing advice; his spirit will be missed. Thanks to the citizens of Orofino, who humbled me with their kindness, especially Tommy and Kathy. John Garrick, who tells me he is hunting again, with his grandson now, I thank you for sharing your words. Thanks to the rest of the gang at Farm Out and beyond: Tom, Lowell, Marcia, Barb, Fran, Mary, Nancy—you continue to inspire me.

Early reader Morgen van Vorst reviewed the plans and

gave sage advice. Zach Slobig, who at least cracked a beer with me on the worksite, kept me company when the clearing job got particularly ugly. Nate Johnson and Heather Smith, two fine writers, got in there and hacked away some unsightly shrubbery. Thanks to Rebecca Solnit, who in one phone conversation showed me a part of the forest I didn't know existed. Friends like Dorrit Gershunt and Lisa Margonelli made me feel like I wasn't alone in the woods. For the smell of fresh coffee and lots of laughs, thank you, my officemates. Also, Helen and Matthew, who inspired me to get serious about getting pregnant, I salute you.

My mom, who taught me the importance of stories, has been understanding and supportive no matter how gnarly things started to look: I love you. My sister, Riana, I literally could not have done this without you—thank you. Though Frannie won't remember any of it, I did some of my best thinking while sitting on a yoga ball, bouncing her to sleep. My dear sweet Bill, my campmate in the wilderness, you are still my best editor, and best friend. Finally, for Dad who gave me that spark that made me believe that anything is possible, I do love you.

Image Credits

Chapter 1. Pat Carpenter

Chapter 2. Pat Carpenter

Chapter 3. Pat Carpenter

Chapter 4. Franklin Schultz

Chapter 5. Pat Carpenter

Chapter 6. Pat Carpenter

Chapter 7. Novella Carpenter

Chapter 8. Pat Carpenter

Chapter 9. U.S. Army

Chapter 10. Pat Carpenter

Chapter 11. Novella Carpenter

Chapter 12. Pat Carpenter

Chapter 13. Pat Carpenter

Chapter 14. Riana Lagarde

Epilogue. Bill Jacobs